# Wilderness Ranger Cookbook

## A Collection of Backcountry Recipes by U.S. Forest Service Wilderness Rangers

Valerie Brunell and Ralph Swain

FALCON

Cover photo by Eric Wunrow.

Printed in Canada.

ISBN 1-56044-038-4

For a free catalog listing Falcon Press books and calendars, please
write to Falcon Press, P.O. Box 1718, Helena, Montana 59624
or call toll-free 1-800-582-2665

♻ Text pages printed on recyled paper

This book was produced through a cooperative venture between the Forest Service, USDA, Coleman Outdoor Products, Inc. and the San Juan National Forest Association.

Additional books and materials about the San Juan National Forest are available through the San Juan National Forest Association. Membership in the Association supports the educational and interpretive programs of the forest. For more information, contact:

**San Juan National Forest Association**
**P.O. Box 2261**
**Durango, Colorado 81302**
**(303) 385-1210**

Proceeds from this book will help train seasonal wilderness rangers.

# CONTENTS

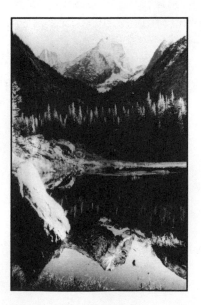

# DEDICATION

---

This cookbook is dedicated to all Forest Service seasonal wilderness rangers and volunteers who have given their hearts and souls to protecting America's wildlands.

The recipes included in this book are theirs - made with care, seasoned with experience and perfected over time.

---

# RECOGNITION

The development of this book was paid for in part by a grant from Coleman Outdoor Products Inc. and Peak One.

**Concept**: Ralph Swain, Interpretive Services
**Editor**: Valerie Brunell
**Artwork**: Tom McMurray and Dick Ostergaard
San Juan National Forest
Durango, Colorado

**Photographs by Tom McMurray,
Durango, Colorado**

Cartoons by Jon R. Herman
Illustrations of John Muir, Aldo Leopold and Howard Zahniser by Linda Reilly

Special thanks to Anne Fege, Lee Carr, Dave Cole, Pat Reed, Dave Porter, Garry Oye, Judy Fraser, Laura Lantz, Scott Edwards, Helen Seidle, Tracey McInerney, Renée Rust and Betty Preston for their help on this book.

# ABOUT THIS BOOK

Sometimes dreams come true.

Two years ago the Rocky Mountain Region of the U.S. Forest Service held a wilderness ranger workshop in Granby, Colorado. The three-day training session brought seasonal and permanent wilderness staff together to exchange ideas about vexing management problems. Participants also practiced primitive skills, such as cutting with an ax and cross-cut saw (chain saws are prohibited in wilderness) and packing with horses and llamas.

As an extra activity, rangers brought campstoves to cook their favorite backcountry meals. This "cookoff" turned out to be one of the highlights of the workshop.

The Wilderness Ranger Cookbook is a compilation of several winning recipes from this workshop as well as a host of others from rangers across the country. These rangers also submitted personal wilderness philosophies to explain their dedication to the job.

Wilderness tips are sprinkled throughout the book to help you, the reader, do your part to preserve America's wildlands. The 1964 Wilderness Act is included in its entirety for your reference.

We hope you enjoy this book as much as we do.

Valerie Brunell    Ralph Swain

"I try to teach people to enjoy the area with an appropriate respect for its integrity as an ecosystem that is complete without human presence - we are just privileged guests. Wilderness to me should exist primarily for its own importance to the earth, not for any 'use' it may have to humanity."
- **Monique H. Slipher, Baker, OR**

## Backcountry Scones

Monique H. Slipher, 5 seasons,
North Fork John Day Wilderness

2 c. flour

2 c. oats

2 tbsp. sugar

1 tsp. salt

2 tsp. baking soda

1/2 c. oil

1 c. milk or 1/2 c. powdered milk
    mixed with 1 c. water

1/2 c. raisins, sunflower seeds, currants, nuts or other filling

water

**In the field:** Mix all ingredients (use 1/2 c. powdered milk mixed with water) except oil. Then add oil. Pat into a well-greased frying pan and score into sections. Cover and cook over low heat until done - 20 min.

**To prepare at home:** Mix dry ingredients together. Blend in oil with a fork until mixture looks like fine crumbs. Add 1 c. milk and pat into a large circle about 1/2-inch thick. Cut into small pieces and place on greased cookie sheet; bake 10-15 min. at 425° until golden brown.

# Blueberry Breakfast Cake

Wendy Reinmuth, 8 seasons,
Maroon Bells-Snowmass Wilderness

*8 oz. Oregon blueberries*
*2 c. Bisquick Mix*
*1/4 c. powdered milk*
*2 tbsp. sugar*
*dash of cinnamon*
*water*

"Wilderness land is unique and valuable. We have an obligation to allow it to sustain itself and manage our own human impacts. How could we exist without it?"
**- Wendy Reinmuth, Aspen, CO**

Heat blueberries. While heating, mix Bisquick, powdered milk, sugar and cinnamon with enough water to make a thick batter. Drop large spoonfuls of batter onto the blueberries. Cover and let cook until the batter has become cake-like.

• **John Muir (1838-1914) -** Nationalist, writer, founding president of Sierra Club. Early advocate of protecting public lands.

"The Greek philosopher Pythagoras said, 'If there be light, then there is darkness; if cold, then heat; if height, depth also; if solid, then fluid; hardness and softness; roughness and smoothness; calm and tempest; prosperity and adversity; life and death.' Wilderness and civilization can be contrasted in the same way. They are opposites."
- Larry A. Jarvinen, Manistee, MI

# Easy Granola

Larry A. Jarvinen, 22 seasons,
Nordhouse Dunes Wilderness

*6 c. rolled oats*
*2 c. grated or pre-shredded coconut*
*2 c. nuts, chopped (any kind - almonds, cashews, walnuts)*
*2/3 c. sesame seeds or sunflower seeds*
*2/3 c. bran flakes*
*2/3 c. wheat germ*
*1/2 c. vegetable oil*
*1/2 c. honey (or molasses, sorghum or maple syrup)*
*1 c. dried fruit*

**To prepare at home:** Roast each of the first six ingredients above separately in a 300° oven until lightly toasted. Combine. Stir in oil and honey thoroughly. Roast in oven at 250° until golden brown. Store in airtight container.
**In the field:** Add dried fruit. Stir and serve with milk.

**Sun Dried Granola:** In a big bowl, put 5 c. oatmeal. In separate bowl, combine 1/2 c. honey, 1/2 c. hot water, 1/2 c. oil, 2 tsp. vanilla. Add this to oatmeal. Then add 1 c. sunflower seeds, 1 c. sesame seeds, 1 c. flax seeds, 1 c. grated coconut, 3/4 c. chopped dried fruit. Mix well and spread flat to dry (at least two days). Serve with milk when ready.

# Egg in the Nest

Walter (Sym) Terhune, 10 seasons,
Whisker Lake Wilderness

*1 piece of bread per serving*
*1 egg per serving*
*1 tbsp. bacon grease, butter or short-
ening*

Over moderate heat, melt
grease, butter or shortening in fry
pan. Grease should cover bottom
of pan. Cut out a hole in center of
bread the size of an egg yolk. Place
bread in pan of hot grease. Break
egg over hole in bread and pour
out egg yolk to sit in hole. Fry the
egg and bread to personal prefer-
ence, flip once and serve.

"To enjoy creation is to enjoy the creator. To enjoy the creator is to know God and view the beauty of His handiwork in creation and in our lives. Wilderness is an experience where we become engulfed in the bond between peace and beauty."
**- Walter (Sym)Terhune, Florence, WI**

**• Aldo Leopold, 1887-1948 -**
Author of the *Sand County Almanac* and leader in early wilderness management.

*Aldo Leopold*
(1887-1948)

# Twigs and Rocks

Rebecca E. Ondov, 1 season,
Scapegoat Wilderness

*4 c. blueberry granola*
*1/4 c. oat bran*
*1/4 c. chopped walnuts*
*4 c. raw quick oats*
*1/4 c. slivered almonds*
*1 c. raisins or currants*
*brown sugar to taste*
*evaporated milk*
*water*

Combine all the ingredients. Add brown sugar and milk to cereal as desired. I prefer to eat it cold, but for a change of pace you can cook it up like hot cereal. Add 1 part cereal to 2/3 part water and heat until warm.

**Variations:** Add dried bananas or peaches.

# Eggs McSanchez

### Jerry Craghead, 12 seasons,
### Holy Cross Wilderness

*2 eggs*
*1 tortilla*
*2 jalapeno peppers, diced*
*Tabasco sauce to taste*
*2 strips of jerky*

**The night before:** Beat the eggs. Tear jerky into little pieces, and peel and chop the jalapenos. Add to eggs. Then add enough Tabasco to extinguish any flames caused by the jalapenos. Mix and let it sit overnight.

**The morning of:** Cook all of the runny stuff over low heat in a pan until it's well done. Scoop it into the tortilla, add a little more Tabasco and hit the trail.

"When viewing the Glen Canyon after the dam was built, Edward Abbey said, 'Once it was different there. I know, I was one of the lucky few.' When I view the wilderness, I say, 'I am one of the lucky few. I will keep it different here.'"
**- Jerry Craghead, Burns, CO**

### Howard Zahniser
(1906-1964)

• **Howard Zahniser (1906-1964)** - Executive Director of the Wilderness Society. He proposed the first wilderness bill in 1956.

# BREAKFAST

> "My personal wilderness philosophy? Do it with flair!"
> **- Dave Atwood, Orleans, CA**

## Griddle Cakes

Dave Atwood, 20 seasons,
Marble Mountain Wilderness

*1 1/4 c. sifted flour*
*2 tsp. baking powder*
*1/2 tsp. soda*
*1 tbsp. sugar*
*1/2 tsp. salt*
*1 beaten egg*
*1 c. buttermilk*
*2 tbsp. oil or melted shortening*

Mix dry ingredients. Mix in egg, buttermilk and oil just until moistened. Batter will be thick and lumpy. Pour on an ungreased griddle, approx. 1/4 c. at a time. Cook over medium heat until brown. Flip. Cook until done and serve.

## New Granola - Jamie Style

Michael McCurdy, 2 seasons,
Moose Plains National Wildlife Refuge

3 *three-inch squares of shredded wheat*
1 1/2 c. *margarine*
1 c. *peanut butter*
1/2 c. *oats*
1/2 c. *sunflower seeds*
1/4 c. *peanuts*
1/4 c. *assorted favorite nuts or cashews*
1/2 c. *raisins*
1 *tsp. cinnamon*
1/3-1/2 c. *powdered milk*
3/4 c. *honey or sugar*

Melt margarine in large pan. Brown shredded wheat. Add oats and brown. Mix in peanut butter, honey or sugar, powdered milk and raisins. Cook over medium heat and stir frequently until raisins bulge. Add nuts, sunflower seeds and cinnamon (sometimes I brown nuts separately). If it's too dry, add more margarine or milk.

"Inspired people can change the world. This world needs a lot of change. By preserving pieces of our past in wilderness, maybe we can find inspiration and vital information to help mend the torn earth."
- Michael McCurdy, Seward, AK

# BREAKFAST

## Superstition Surprise

Greg F. Hansen, 11 seasons,
Superstition Wilderness

2 c. oatmeal, instant or slow cooking
1/3 c. raisins
1/3 c. favorite mixed, chopped nuts
1/2 c. brown sugar
1/4 tsp. cinnamon,
1/4 tsp. nutmeg
1/4 tsp. allspice
3/4 c. powdered milk, optional
water

Mix all ingredients in a ziplock bag before hitting the trail. When the breakfast bell rings... pour boiling water over a bowl of your Superstition Surprise and cover the pot. Wait approximately 2 min. and you're ready to chow down. Makes 3-4 servings.

## Sunrise Oatmeal

Don Duff, 3 seasons,
Deseret Peak Wilderness

*3/4 c. oatmeal*
*1/4 c. dried bananas or raisins*
*cinnamon to taste*
*1 tbsp. powdered milk*
*1/4 c. chopped apple, optional*
*1 c. water*

Add ingredients to water. Bring to a boil, reduce heat and cook for 2 min. Serve.

"Wilderness reflects the different cultures of man. We must not lose our love for this land as it provides for our health, well being and self-renewal. To understand wilderness and marvel at its beauty and value is to understand ourselves."
- **Don Duff, Salt Lake City, UT**

## Wilderness facts:

• The Wilderness Act was signed into law September 3, 1964 by President Lyndon B. Johnson. Photo courtesy of National Archives.

# The Eagle Cap Club

Jim Bradley, 10 seasons,
Eagle Cap Wilderness

*1 dry salami, the hottest and spiciest you can find*
*1 lb. sharp cheddar cheese*
*1 box of your favorite crackers*

This is my favorite trail lunch. It's fast, easy and tasty. Slice the cheese and salami. Place between two crackers to make a sandwich. The ingredients can easily survive a ten-day hike in the heat. This is named in honor of the Eagle Cap Wilderness where this sandwich has kept me alive for years.

"Wilderness is a pathway to truth. The more time we spend in the wilderness, the more we learn about what is really significant about life and ourselves. Wilderness gives us a clear-eyed perspective free of clutter. Life's major decisions should be made in the mountains, the desert, the forests or in any other wild place."
- Jim Bradley, Enterprise, OR

## Wilderness facts:

- Wilderness is managed by the U.S. Forest Service, the National Park Service, the Fish and Wildlife Service and the Bureau of Land Management.
- Nationwide, there are over 500 wilderness areas totaling 96 million acres, or 4 percent of all U.S. land.
- The largest wilderness area is the 8.7 million-acre Wrangell - St. Elias National Park in Alaska.
- The largest wilderness outside of Alaska is the 2.3 million-acre Frank Church-River of No Return Wilderness in Idaho.
- The smallest wilderness is the 5-acre Oregon Islands.

# Bagel Break

Becky Boyer, 4 seasons,
Big Island Lake Wilderness

*1 bagel*
*1 pkg. cream cheese*
*1 cucumber, thinly sliced*
*1 handful alfalfa sprouts*

Cut bagel in half. Spread cream cheese over both halves, using amount to satisfy personal taste. Place cucumber slices and alfalfa sprouts on top and enjoy.

"Everyone benefits from wilderness, even those who may have never set foot in one. So it's important that everyone understand it needs to be protected and preserved."
- Becky Boyer, Munising, MI

## Memorable words in wilderness:

"It is not good for man to be kept perforce at all times in the presence of his species. Solitude, in the sense of being often alone, is essential to any depth of meditation or of character; and solitude in the presence of natural beauty and grandeur is the cradle of thoughts and aspirations which are not only good for the individual but which society could ill do without."
- **John Stuart Mill,** *Principles of Political Economy*

# Sautéed Chanterelles

William DellaRocco, 2 seasons,
Lizard Head Wilderness

"We should begin to rethink our priorities, renew our commitment to preserving our wildernesses from unalterable damages and restore our public image to that of the caretakers of our forests."
- **William DellaRocco, Dolores, CO**

*2 handfuls of chanterelles*
*1/2 clove of garlic, chopped fine*
*1/4 onion, diced*
*dash of soy sauce, optional*

Cook chanterelles, onions and garlic on low heat. The key to not overcooking this delicate mushroom is to continually remove the pan from the cookstove. If the garlic is turning brown or the onions are smoking, snatch the dish from heat. Slowly fry until the chanterelles soften. Add soy sauce and serve.

## Mushroom identification:

- Accuracy of identification is essential in order not to confuse a poisonous mushroom with an edible one.
- Be meticulous when identifying. If in doubt, don't eat it.
- Only eat healthy mushrooms.
- Mushrooms should always be cooked before eating.
- When trying a new kind, eat only a small amount and save a few raw pieces in case of a misidentification.
- Only eat one type at a time.
- Remember that different people can have different reactions to the same mushroom.

# Let'seatus
# Some Boletus
# (Sautéed Mushrooms)

Bill C. Self, 25 seasons,
High Uintas Wilderness

*1 c. sliced boletus mushrooms (use
canned mushrooms if not
familiar with wild varieties)*
*1 stick butter*
*4 oz. V-8 juice*
*salt, pepper, garlic powder to taste*
*2 dashes of red wine*
*2-4 slices french bread*

Brush the organic debris from the mushrooms and peel the pores from the undersurface of the cap. Then slice them vertically in about 1/4-inch layers. Heat up the pan until the butter is barely sizzling. Sauté the mushrooms for about 2 min., turning them as they begin to darken. Add V-8, spices and wine. Stir while cooking for 2 min. Do not overcook. Use sauce leftover for dipping french bread.

"Many years ago I discovered the presence of something very wonderful in the forest. It gives me peace of mind unlike anything else in my life. I've spent many an hour listening and thinking to whatever this is and still cannot describe it to mere mortals. They'll have to discover it for themselves. But then again, I'm afraid most major organized religions would go bankrupt if everyone found out what really exists in the wilderness."
- Bill C. Self, Ogden, UT

**Note:** When selecting mushrooms, make sure you know what you are doing. The boletus mushrooms have pores under the cap rather than gills.They have a large crown (golden/brown with a slight white cracking in the mature stages). The stem is whitish-grey with slight feathering. The buttons are best for eating, but are the host for a small fly so they must be carefully cleaned to avoid maggots.

## Vitamin Balls

Bob Oset, 25 seasons,
Selway-Bitterroot Wilderness

*1 c. honey*
*1 c. peanut butter*
*1/2 c. wheat germ*
*1 c. soymilk powder*
*1/2 c. carob powder*
*1 c. sesame seeds*

**To prepare at home:** Mix all ingredients together. Separate into bite-size pieces and chill. Store in an airtight container and hit the trail.

# Bongko Bean Spread

Yvonne Schmidt, 4 seasons,
Boundary Waters Canoe Area Wilderness

1 1/4 c. cooked garbanzo beans
1/4 tsp. parsley
1/4 tsp. chili powder
1/8 tsp. cumin
1/8 tsp. salt
dash of garlic
vegetable oil

**To prepare at home:** Mash garbanzos or put through a food mill, ricer, or blender until they make a paste. Add spices and stir well. Store in airtight, heavy plastic container. Eat with crackers or chips. If the bean spread seems too dry, add a little vegetable oil.

"I became a wilderness ranger because I wanted to play a part in the 'on-the-ground' management of this beautiful lake country wilderness and to know firsthand its mystique and appreciate its wonders and challenges."
- Yvonne Schmidt,
Cook, MN

## Special conditions of the Wilderness Act:
• Aircraft or motorboat use is permitted where established prior to designation as a wilderness.
• Livestock grazing may continue where established prior to designation as a wilderness.
• Hunting, fishing and trapping are allowed under State and Federal laws, although hunting is prohibited in most national parks.
• Outfitting and guiding services are accepted under special use permits that meet wilderness purposes.

# Pilaf de Résistance

Jon R. Herman, 2 seasons,
Alpine Lakes Wilderness

1 c. quick brown rice
1/2 c. instant refried beans
2 1/4 c. water
1 sm. can chicken or turkey meat
1 slice cheddar cheese
1/4 c. diced green pepper
1/4 c. chopped celery
2 tbsp. diced onion
1/2 tsp. diced garlic or garlic powder
1 tsp. dried celery
1/4 tsp. salt

Bring water to a boil. Add rice. Cover and simmer for 10 minutes. Then add all ingredients except cheese. Simmer and stir occasionally for 5 min. Add cheese and set aside with cover on. Serve when cheese is melted.

"As a species, our roots are in wilderness. It's a reservoir of clean air, clear water, fish and wildlife, serenity, beauty and reality. It wakes us up from the confused, dreamy mental state our society inspires. We need wilderness and we need to save and preserve what we have left - not only for ourselves, but as a long-overdue acknowledgement of the right of other living things to live their own lives for themselves."
- Jon R. Herman, Ellensburg, WA

## Preparing for your trip:
- When buying packs, clothing and tents, select colors that blend with the natural surroundings.
- Obtain information about various areas and regulations governing their use well ahead of time.
- Repackage food in plastic bags or other light weight containers. Avoid packing cans into the wilderness. And remember, if you pack it in, pack it out.

# DINNER

"Wilderness is for the use of the public, but not necessarily unrestricted use. To the best of our ability, we as managers need to do what is necessary to protect it. "
- **R. Patrick Cook, Darrington, WA**

# Hobo Stew

R. Patrick Cook, 11 seasons,
Boulder River Wilderness

1 pkg. Lipton soup, any flavor
1/2 onion
1/2 zucchini
1 jalapeno pepper
1 handful of spinach noodles
1 can of boneless chicken
1 stalk of celery
curry powder, allspice, celery seed, red
    pepper - one tad of each except
    curry which gets 3.
3 c. water

Boil soup in 3 c. water. Add noodles and chicken. While the soup is coming to a boil, add vegetables slowly. Stir frequently. Once all vegetables are in and soup has returned to a boil, turn off and cover for 5-15 min. Add spices and serve. This recipe can easily be improvised, but it always turns out good and reasonably healthy for you.

# Pig's Ass Chili

Art Marcilla, 6 seasons,
South San Juan Wilderness

1 lb. diced pork
1/2 onion
4 oz. green chili, fresh or canned
1/2 c. cheddar cheese, optional
1 tbsp. flour
1 tomato, fresh or canned
garlic, salt and pepper to taste
1/3 c. water

"I am committed to preservation of the land. The present wilderness ethics outlined in the Wilderness Act place more muscle in the preservation of certain lands. What a great idea."
- **Art Marcilla, Monte Vista, CO**

Cube and brown meat in skillet (drain out excess grease). Add onion and brown lightly. Add flour and brown. Add water, tomato, green chili and spices. Simmer for about 20 minutes. Spread slices of cheese over top. Let melt and serve.

## No trace wilderness tips:
- Stay on designated trails.
- Avoid cutting switchbacks.
- When traveling cross country, select rocky ground or forested areas where your tracks will not be seen.
- When traveling cross country in a group, spread out to avoid trampling.
- Leave no trace of your visit once you're gone.

## Six Grain Casserole

Keith Sprengel, 10 years,
Columbia Wilderness

"I grew up playing in the hardwood forests of the Midwest. Becoming a wilderness ranger seemed a logical progression of the life I loved as a child. Everyone needs to work to expand and protect our wilderness system in a truly untrammeled, pristine condition."

- **Keith Sprengel, Troutdale, OR**

*1/8 c. bulgar wheat*
*1/8 c. brown rice*
*1/8 c. millet*
*1/8 c. soy grits*
*1/8 c. wheat berries*
*1/8 c. barley*
*2 tsp. spice mix*
*water*

Combine all grains and simmer in water for 30 minutes. Add spices, mix and serve. If we're talking deluxe camp, add cheese and veggies of your choice. Makes 2 servings.

**To make spice mix:** Combine equal parts of curry, salt, pepper, summer savory, thyme, wild seasons and garlic powder.

## Selecting a campsite:

- Select either a well-established campsite if you are in a popular location or a previously-unused site if you are in a remote location.
- If using an existing site, concentrate the use where damage has already occurred.
- If camping in an unused site, spread out activities. Stay off fragile plants and disperse your use over a wide area.
- If in a remote location, select a site away from trails, lakes, streams and other campsites.

# Veggies and Pots

Lee Kirsch, 9 seasons,
Mount Massive Wilderness

*1 1/2 c. dried potatoes*
*1 1/2 c. dried veggies - zucchini, bell*
*    peppers, spinach, onions, mush-*
*    rooms*
*1/2 c. powdered milk*
*1 pkg. noodle/chicken cup-a-soup*
*oregano, garlic powder, chili powder*
*    and salt to taste*
*1/2 to 3/4 c. grated cheddar cheese*
*Parmesan cheese*
*water*

"My personal wilderness philosophy is to preserve this natural/recreational resource for everyone to use and hopefully in the best, most efficient way."
**- Lee Kirsch, Leadville, CO**

Put all ingredients, except cheeses and spices, in pot with enough water to cover. Cook on medium to high heat, stirring occasionally, until potatoes and veggies are soft. Add seasonings to taste. Sprinkle with cheddar and Parmesan cheese and serve. Fresh vegetables may be substituted for dried ones and in any combination as desired.

> "I believe wilderness should be maintained in such a way as to preserve it for future generations so that people can see what land looks like without man's influence."
> - **Steve Hoots, Yampa, CO**

## Flat Tops Trout

Steve Hoots, 4 seasons,
Flat Tops Wilderness

*4 medium fish*
*2 c. pancake batter*
*2 tbsp. vegetable oil*
*salt, pepper and lemon pepper to taste*
*water*

Catch 4 medium fish using your favorite flies or lures. Mix pancake batter with water according to directions on package. Heat skillet with vegetable oil (it should be hot enough to bead water). Dip fish in batter. Turning fish often, cook until batter is browned. Add seasonings to taste and serve.

---

## Campstoves:

• Whenever possible, use a campstove instead of building a fire. Campstoves are more efficient for cooking, while campfires sterilize the soil and make unsightly scars on the land.

# Tofu Curry

Jan Brittain, 5 seasons,
Mokelumne Wilderness

*1 sm. bell pepper*
*1 sm. onion*
*8 oz. vacuum-packed tofu*
*1 pkg. curry and shell pasta mix (If unavailable, 1 c. whole wheat pasta shells, 2 tbsp. dried peas, 1 tsp. red pepper and curry to taste will serve as a substitute.)*
*2 tbsp. oil*
*1 1/4 c. water*
*dried pineapple, raw coconut, raisins, and peanuts to taste*

Dice bell pepper and onion and sauté in oil until soft. Add cubed tofu and sauté for a few more min. Add water and curry pasta mix. Bring to boil. Lower heat and cook 20 min. Top with pineapple, coconut, raisins and peanuts and enjoy.

"I became a wilderness ranger because I like the idea of having the mountains for my office, and I like working intimately with the spirit of the wilderness."
- **Jan Brittain, Pollock Pines, CA**

---

## Wilderness management:

• Wilderness areas are administered for the use and enjoyment of the American people so long as the areas are left unimpaired for future use and enjoyment.
• Management of wilderness prohibits the use of motor vehicles, mechanical transport and motorized equipment except in emergencies.
• Permanent or temporary roads are not permitted.

"Our wilderness areas represent a priceless natural heritage, the last remnants of wild America in a sea of humanity and with it, 'progress' and development. The work wilderness rangers do is crucial. For without them, the wild in wilderness would be destroyed by thoughtless people."
- **Eric Horstman,** **Weaverville, CA**

## Tortellini a la Trinity Alps

Eric Horstman, 3 seasons,
Trinity Alps Wilderness

*7 oz. pkg. tortellini*
*8 oz. tomato sauce*
*2 shallots, diced*
*4 mushrooms, diced*
*cheese, oregano, salt, pepper to taste*
*water*

Add tortellini to pot of boiling water and cook for 10-15 min. until tortellini is soft and filling no longer crunchy. Take pot off stove and drain all but a couple of teaspoons of water. Add tomato sauce, shallots, and mushrooms and simmer over low heat for 2-4 min. Season to taste with cheese, oregano, salt and pepper. Serves 2.

## Memorable words in wilderness:

"Something will have gone out of us as a people if we ever let the remaining wilderness be destroyed."
- **Wallace Stegner,** Pulitzer Prize winner

## Pep Jack Stew

John M. Brandon, 9 seasons,
Absaroka-Beartooth Wilderness

1 c. noodles (any kind)
1 handful dried veggies (onions, green
    peppers, tomatoes)
dash of cooking oil
dash of garlic powder
2 oz. of Monterey Pepper Jack Cheese
1/2 c. dried shrimp
water

Boil 3-4 c. water (more if you want soup). Add dried veggies, oil and garlic. Let simmer for 5 min. Add dried shrimp. Add noodles and cook until done. Drain broth (soup in a cup) or leave in. Grate cheese and mix in. It's quick and it's spicy.

"Wilderness is a part of the planet that is valued for itself - no strings attached. Its beauty and inaccessibility give it a quality of 'manlessness', yet I feel comfortable being there. Mainly I walk lightly and am there to enjoy, not destroy."
- **John M. Brandon, Bozeman, MT**

"I became a wilderness ranger because I enjoy backpacking and because I like a challenge."
- **Lisa M. Applebee, Cobalt, ID**

# Chicken-Rice Curry

Lisa M. Applebee, 1 season,
Frank Church-River of No Return Wilderness

*1/2 c. instant rice*
*1/4 c. raisins*
*4 tbsp. margarine*
*4 c. water*
*1 pkg. chicken noodle soup*
*2 tbsp. curry*
*1 sm. can of chicken*

Sauté rice and raisins in margarine. Add water, chicken soup and curry. Bring to boil. Simmer for 15 min. When almost done, stir in chicken. Heat until warm.

---

## Campfires:
- If you must build a fire in a new place, choose a site in mineral soil.
- Build campfires away from meadows, trees, logs and boulders.
- Keep fires small. Collect only dead or downed wood. Burn all wood to ashes.
- Never leave a fire unattended. Extinguish the fire by drowning it with water so that it is cold to the touch.
- Be sure to camouflage site before you leave.

## Pita Pizza

Ted Scroggin, 7 seasons,
High Uintas Wilderness

3-4 pita or pocket bread
6 oz. can tomato paste
1/4 tsp. oregano
salt and pepper to taste
1/2-1 clove of garlic
1/4 c. chopped onion
4 whole mushrooms
1 handful of chopped bell peppers
1 scallion, chopped
1/2 c. of favorite cheese, grated
1/2 c. water
2 tbsp. butter

Combine tomato paste, water, garlic, oregano, salt and pepper over medium heat. In another pan, sauté mushrooms, bell pepper, onions and scallions in butter for a few minutes. Combine with sauce. In another pan, place one pita bread. Spread with sauce, top with cheese. Cover with lid and heat until cheese begins to melt. Remove and enjoy.

" Once you have made the effort to travel into the wilderness, if nothing else, enjoy the immense beauty and the ever-changing weather."
- **Ted Scroggin, Park City, UT**

"I became a
wilderness ranger
because of my
total fascination
with the patterns
of nature,
whether it be
leaves in the
groundcover,
lichens on the
rock or clouds in
the sky. Benign
neglect is not a
wilderness
management
strategy."
- Judith Fraser,
Cle Elum, WA

# Marinated Green Beans

Judith Fraser, 9 seasons,
Alpine Lakes Wilderness

*2 c. fresh green beans*
*1 sm. shallot, onion or green onion,*
*   chopped*
*1 clove of garlic, minced*
*2 tbsp. vinegar*
*3 tbsp. olive oil*
*1 tbsp. mixed herbs - oregano, basil,*
*   chevril, dill*
*1 tbsp. honey*
*1/4 tbsp. dry mustard, optional*
*ground pepper to taste*

Steam beans until they are just tender. Then put everything in a container and mix. Double bag, zip-loc or poly bottle can be used for storing beans.

## Cous-cous and Veggies

Patricia Cohn, 6 seasons,
Pecos Wilderness

*1/2 c. cous-cous*
*1 1/4 c. water*
*1/2 c. dried veggies, any kind*
*vegetable broth, lemon, ramen season-*
*ing to taste*

Boil water. Add dried veggies and cook for 2 or 3 min. Add cous-cous and remove from heat. Cover and let sit for 5 min. Add seasonings and serve. Makes 2 cups. You can also use fresh vegetables, but it takes longer to cook.

"Wilderness is more than lines on a map. It is also an attitude. This attitude reflects the thought that the earth and its community of life exist for its own sake, as opposed to being for the benefit of man. Wilderness gives us the opportunity to reflect on the role of humankind as a part of the community of life, rather than as a conqueror of nature."
**- Patricia Cohn, Pecos, NM**

## Spanish Rice with Stir-Fry Veggies

Janice Chapman, 10 seasons,
La Garita Wilderness

"My parents, grandparents and uncle instilled in me a great love and respect for the land. The feeling of happiness and peace of mind that comes from the beauty of nature is so very precious. We need to protect our wilderness."
- Janice Chapman, Gunnison, CO

1 tbsp. oil
1 sm. red onion, diced
3 sm. yellow summer squash, sliced
1 green pepper, diced
1 pkg. dried Spanish rice
2 sm. cans spicy hot V-8 juice
1 c. water
1 c. shredded mozzarella cheese

Add veggies to heated oil and cover loosely with lid. Stir often for about 5 min., then set aside. In a different pan, combine V-8 juice, water and rice and bring to a boil. Let simmer for about 15 min. without lid. Add veggies and stir. Sprinkle cheese on top and cover until melted. Makes 2-4 servings.

. WILDERNESS .
AMERICA'S
RESOURCE
1964 ENDURING 1994

This symbol commemorates the
30th anniversary of the
National Wilderness Preservation System.

## Chicken-Chuck

Charlie Hellen, 33 seasons,
John Muir Wilderness

"Wilderness cannot be under-used, only over-used."

**- Charlie Hellen,** Tollhouse, CA

*3 boneless chicken breasts, halved*
*1 lg. green pepper, sweet*
*1 lg. red pepper, sweet*
*8 oz. can pineapple chunks*
*2 oz. apple juice*
*1 lg. red onion*
*1 c. minute rice*
*olive oil*
*water*

In large skillet, brown lightly both sides of chicken breasts in olive oil. Add pineapple juice and chunks from can. Ring cut onion and peppers. Add to skillet along with apple juice. Cover and simmer over medium heat for 20 min. Meanwhile, boil water. Add rice, turn down heat and let simmer until rice is soft. Serve chicken over bed of rice.

---

## Memorable words in wilderness:

"We abuse the land because we regard it as a commodity belonging to us. When we see land as a community to which we belong, we may begin to use it with love and respect."
                    **- Aldo Leopold,** wilderness advocate

# Alpine Tortellini with Pesto Sauce

Rob Bleiberg, 3 seasons,
Eagles Nest Wilderness

*instant pesto sauce*
*8 or 10 oz. pkg. tortellini - make*
*sure you get kind that doesn't*
*need to be refrigerated*
*2 tbsp. butter*
*1/2 oz. Parmesan cheese*
*1 oz. pine nuts or unsalted*
*cashews*
*water*

Bring pot of water to a boil. Add tortellini, reduce heat and cover. When tortellini is soft, leave covered and set aside. In another pan, melt butter and add pesto sauce (use instructions on pesto sauce package). Drain tortellini and add pesto sauce and nuts. Sprinkle with Parmesan cheese.

## No trace wilderness tips:
- Avoid trenching around your tent.
- Stay only a short time in any one place.
- On undisturbed sites, move your tent every day.
- Avoid building camp structures.
- Wash dishes, clothes and yourself away from stream or lake.
- Cover latrines thoroughly before breaking camp.
- Pick up every bit of trash and pack it out.

# Ginger Desperation over Rice

Nate Inouye, 3 seasons,
Mount Zirkel Wilderness

"I chose to be a wilderness ranger to get back to the mountains I love."
- **Nate Inouye, Steamboat Springs, CO**

*1/2 lb. hamburger*
*2 tbsp. grated ginger root*
*1 c. chopped broccoli*
*1 c. chopped cauliflower*
*1/2 lemon*
*honey*
*soy sauce*
*1 c. rice*
*water*

Rinse rice. Put in covered pot with 2 c. water. Bring to boil at high heat. Turn stove down and simmer until done (20-40 min. depending on stove and altitude). Brown hamburger in large covered pot over medium heat. Drain excess grease. Add ginger root, broccoli, cauliflower and simmer over low heat 5-10 min. (vegetables should remain crisp). Squeeze lemon over it and mix. Add honey and soy sauce to taste. Serve over hot rice. Makes 2 hearty servings.

# Snowmass Trout

Walter Werner, 30 seasons,
Maroon Bells - Snowmass Wilderness

*4 legally caught trout*
*10 slices of bacon*
*10 oz. stuffed green olives*
*2 cloves of garlic*
*1/3 c. corn meal*
*1/3 c. Bisquick (or plain flour)*
*1/2 tsp. corn starch*
*black pepper to taste*

Mix corn meal, Bisquick, corn starch and pepper. After catching and cleaning four 8- to 10-inch trout (release any trout over 12 inches), fry bacon until chewy. Remove bacon and set aside. Heat green olives in bacon grease. Slice garlic and place equal amounts in fish body cavity. Roll fish in pre-mixed corn meal. Slice chewy bacon into two-inch strips and wrap around olives. Re-fry until bacon is more crisp. Remove wrapped olives and fry fish until golden brown. While frying the fish, enjoy the wrapped olives as hors d'oeuvres.

# Burrito Power

Ralph Swain, 10 seasons,
Indian Peaks Wilderness

8 oz. can refried beans
2 whole jalapeno peppers - the hotter
    the better
6 oz. can of whole kernel corn
3 oz. can diced black olives
3 oz. salsa
3 oz. yogurt or sour cream
grated swiss cheese
1 pkg. whole wheat burrito shells

Combine beans, sliced peppers, corn and olives. Cook until warm. Remove and cover. In skillet, warm burrito shells. Spread mixture onto shells. Sprinkle with cheese. Fold shell over and heat until cheese melts. Then top with yogurt or sour cream and salsa. Serve. Continue process until everyone screams enough! Makes 4 servings.

**Hint:** Put the first four ingredients in a container the night before to let flavors blend.

"I spent 10 seasons working as a seasonal wilderness ranger. Camping out under the stars, meeting people from all walks of life and sharing the land ethic has made this the best job one could ever have."
**- Ralph Swain, Granby, CO**

"Wilderness provides me with mental, physical and spiritual healing, but overuse and over-crowding are threatening that. I think we should put much more emphasis on preservation and less on providing recreation."
- Sharon Napp, Skykomish, WA

# Red Lentil Glop

Sharon Napp, 4 seasons,
Henry M. Jackson Wilderness

*2 sm. handfuls of red lentils*
*1 sm. handful sunflower seeds*
*1 or 2 handfuls of dried onions, mush-rooms and zuchinni*
*pepper, garlic powder, cayenne pepper and onion powder to taste*
*cheese, any kind, cut in sm. chunks*
*water*

Bring water to a boil. Add all ingredients except cheese (if using fresh veggies, add them after 5 min.). Boil until lentils are reasonably soft - 6-8 min. Remove from heat. Pour out excess water. Add cheese and stir until melted. Shovel into mouth with a trusty spoon.

---

## Be considerate of others:

• Keep pets under control at all times. If possible, leave them at home.
• Keep noise at acceptable levels while hiking or camping. Loud noises can spook wildlife and infringe on others' solitude.

# Mountain Brook Trout

Rich Hamilton, 2 seasons,
Weminuche Wilderness

1 brook trout
2 tbsp. butter
1 tsp. lemon
1 tsp. garlic, *add more to taste*
1/2 tsp. dill weed
3 bacon strips

"I learned how to live off the land when I was young and I had a sense of my own wilderness ethic long before anyone taught me what I now know and practice today."
**- Rich Hamilton, Creede, CO**

My recipe is simple and delicious. The only difficult part is catching these cunning mountain brook trout. They can easily be caught in small mountain streams with a 1/8-oz. Panter Martin spinning lure or a Black Nymph fly. Light test line and a sneaky upstream approach are most effective.

Once the fish is caught and cleaned, prepare two sheets of tin foil large enough to seal your catch. Add all ingredients and seal tightly. Cook over medium high heat, turning every few min., until sizzling (approx. 20 min.). Bacon fat keeps it from burning.

"Wilderness is a great teacher of living systems - present, past and future - and an outstanding place for personal re-creation and recreation. It demands our care and our respect."
- **Lois Ziemann, Jackson, WY**

# Tortellini with Clams

Lois Ziemann, 2 seasons,
Gros Ventre Wilderness

*8 oz. pkg. tortellini pasta*
*1 sm. can of clams*
*1 c. nonfat dry milk powder - add water and make it thick*
*3 tbsp. hard butter (margarine won't keep as long)*
*1/4 c. green pepper*
*1/4 c. red pepper*
*1/2 c. mushrooms*
*1 red onion, optional*
*Parmesan cheese*
*Italian seasoning to taste - equal parts of oregano, basil, garlic salt, coarse black pepper and a pinch of thyme.*
*water*

Boil tortellini until done. Drain off water. Add butter. When melted, add other ingredients and cook until heated through. (**Note:** if you don't like your veggies crunchy, boil them along with the tortellini.) Makes 2 servings.

---

## Memorable words in wilderness:

"We don't inherit the earth from our ancestors, we borrow it from our children."

**- Unknown**

# Alpine Spaghetti

Tracey McInerney, 5 seasons,
Weminuche Wilderness

1/2 c. pinon nuts
1/2 c. grated Romano cheese
1/4 c. raisins
1/2 tbsp. Italian seasoning - equal
   parts of basil, thyme, oregano,
   garlic
1 tbsp. olive oil or safflower oil
1 handful of spaghetti noodles
water

"Wilderness rangers have the challenging opportunity to encourage the public to participate in preserving wildlands. All wilderness visitors must learn to adjust their needs to nature rather than adjusting nature to their needs."
- **Tracey McInerney, Durango, CO**

Add spaghetti to boiling water. Mix in oil. Cook until soft. Drain water and add rest of ingredients. Heat until warm. This is delicious when served with wild greens or alfalfa sprout salad.

# Backcountry Burritos

Hal Wentz, 2 seasons,
Mount Zirkel Wilderness

*1 pkg. dried refried beans*
*10-12 tortillas*
*hard cheese*
*hot sauce*
*1 head of lettuce*
*1 tomato*
*2 c. water*

Bring 2 c. of water to boil. Add beans. Stir occasionally and let stand 5 min. Put beans, cheese, hot sauce, lettuce and tomatoes on tortillas and eat. Makes 10-12 servings.

---

## Packing with animals:

- Take only the minimum number of animals needed.
- Avoid tying pack animals to trees. If you must tie animals to trees during brief stops, trees should be at least 8 inches in diameter and well away from trails.
- Avoid picketing pack animals. If you must picket, move them frequently.
- Keep tied, picketed and hobbled pack animals well away from trails, camp, lakes and streams.
- Tie, picket or hobble animals only in dry areas to minimize trampling damage.
- When meeting others on your trip, step off lower side of trail and stand still while riders pass.

## Taco Salad

Gregg Heid, 10 seasons,
Indian Peaks Wilderness

*1 can chili con carne*
*3 oz. mild or hot salsa*
*tortilla chips*
*1/2 tomato*
*1/2 sm. onion*
*1/4 head of lettuce*
*grated cheddar cheese*

Heat up chili and salsa on stove. Pour over a plate of crushed tortilla chips, easily obtained by putting them in the bottom of your backpack. Dice up tomato, onion and lettuce. Mix with chips and chili. Cover with grated cheese. Let cheese melt and enjoy.

"Wilderness is the most important thing our country has. We need to designate more as soon as possible so future generations will be able to experience nature at her finest. We must never forget that at one time our whole country was wilderness. Look what's available after only 200 years."
**- Gregg Heid, Granby, CO**

## Packing with animals:

• For long periods, tie pack animals to a hitchline stretched between two sturdy trees.

# Regurgitate de la Prospector con Yama Yama

Julia Becker, 3 seasons,
Lee Metcalf Wilderness

1 c. rice
1/2 c. lentils
1 handful sunflower seeds
1/2 handful flax seeds
15 prunes, pitted
1 tea bag of yama yama barley tea
1 heaping tbsp. margarine
1 handful of seaweed
5-6 large slices of favorite cheese
dash of cayenne, if you like it hot
2 dashes each of lemon thyme, dill,
    basil and sage
water

In water, cook up rice with lentils, prunes and seeds. Once boiling, dip in tea bag for 5-10 min. Then add margarine, seaweed, cayenne and spices. Mix. When rice mixture is near done, add cheese, reduce heat and cover until cheese is melted. Drive spoon through the crust and gorge.

# Chicken Ramen Goulash

Karen L. Bowles, 3 seasons,
Rawah Wilderness

*1 pkg. chicken ramen noodles*
*6 1/2 oz. can of chicken*
*fresh sliced mushrooms, as many as*
*    you want*
*1/2 c. chopped celery*
*any other vegetables, optional*
*salt and pepper to taste*

Make soup according to directions on package. Just before noodles are cooked, add the remaining ingredients and cook until warm. Makes 2 servings.

"Wilderness is a state of mind where you can get back to the basics of life itself, a place to re-evaluate what is important in life, to test values, and discover new facets within yourself. If wilderness should ever disappear, the human race has forever lost its ability to discover life as it has evolved and implications for life in the future."
**- Karen L. Bowles, Stub Creek, CO**

- courtesy of Janet Reeves, Rocky Mountain News

# The National Wilderness

# Preservation System

## Legend

🌲 Wilderness Areas

■ Wilderness Areas less than 20,000 Acres

# WILDERNESS AREAS

## Forest Service Wilderness Areas and Acres

## Alabama

| | |
|---|---|
| Cheaha | 7,490 |
| Sipsey | 25,906 |

## Alaska

| | |
|---|---|
| Admiralty Island | 937,459 |
| Coronation Island | 19,232 |
| Endicott River | 98,729 |
| Maurelle Islands | 4,937 |
| Misty Fjords | 2,142,243 |
| Petersburg Creek-Duncan Salt Chuck | 46,777 |
| Russell Fjord | 348,701 |
| South Baranof | 319,568 |
| South Prince of Wales | 90,996 |
| Stikine-LeConte | 448,841 |
| Tebenkof Bay | 66,839 |
| Tracy Arm-Fords Terror | 653,179 |
| Warren Island | 11,181 |
| West Chichagof-Yakobi | 264,747 |

## Arizona

| | |
|---|---|
| Apache Creek | 5,420 |
| Bear Wallow | 11,080 |
| Castle Creek | 26,030 |
| Cedar Bench | 14,950 |
| Chiricahua | 87,700 |
| Escudilla | 5,200 |
| Fossil Springs | 22,149 |
| Four Peaks | 61,074 |
| Galiuro | 76,317 |
| Granite Mountain | 9,800 |
| Hellsgate | 37,440 |
| Juniper Mesa | 7,600 |
| Kachina Peaks | 18,616 |
| Kanab Creek | 63,760 |
| Kendrick Mountain | 6,510 |
| Mazatzal | 252,390 |
| Miller Peak | 20,190 |
| Mount Baldy | 7,079 |
| Mount Wrightson | 25,260 |
| Munds Mountain | 24,411 |
| Pajarita | 7,420 |
| Pine Mountain | 20,059 |
| Pusch Ridge | 56,933 |
| Red Rock-Secret Mountain | 47,194 |
| Rincon Mountain | 38,590 |
| Saddle Mountain | 40,539 |
| Salome | 18,531 |
| Salt River Canyon | 32,101 |
| Santa Teresa | 26,780 |
| Sierra Ancha | 20,850 |
| Strawberry Crater | 10,743 |
| Superstition | 159,757 |
| Sycamore Canyon | 55,937 |
| West Clear Creek | 15,238 |
| Wet Beaver | 6,155 |
| Woodchute | 5,600 |

## Arkansas

| | |
|---|---|
| Black Fork Mountain | 7,576 |
| Caney Creek | 14,460 |
| Dry Creek | 6,310 |
| East Fork | 10,777 |
| Flatside | 10,105 |
| Hurricane Creek | 15,057 |
| Leatherwood | 16,735 |
| Poteau Mountain | 10,884 |
| Richland Creek | 11,817 |
| Upper Buffalo | 10,984 |

## California

| | |
|---|---|
| Agua Tibia | 15,933 |
| Ansel Adams | 230,258 |
| Bucks Lake | 21,000 |
| Caribou | 20,546 |
| Carson-Iceberg | 158,628 |
| Castle Crags | 8,627 |
| Chanchelulla | 8,200 |
| Cucamonga | 12,781 |

# WILDERNESS AREAS

| | |
|---|---|
| Desolation | 63,475 |
| Dick Smith | 67,800 |
| Dinkey Lakes | 30,000 |
| Dome Land | 93,781 |
| Emigrant | 112,277 |
| Golden Trout | 303,511 |
| Granite Chief | 19,048 |
| Hauser | 7,547 |
| Hoover | 48,601 |
| Ishi | 41,099 |
| Jennie Lakes | 10,289 |
| John Muir | 580,323 |
| Kaiser | 22,700 |
| Machesna Mountain | 19,760 |
| Marble Mountain | 241,744 |
| Mokelumne | 98,921 |
| Monarch | 44,896 |
| Mount Shasta | 33,845 |
| North Fork | 7,999 |
| Pine Creek | 13,480 |
| Red Buttes | 16,150 |
| Russian | 12,000 |
| San Gabriel | 36,118 |
| San Gorgonio | 56,722 |
| San Jacinto | 32,248 |
| San Mateo Canyon | 38,484 |
| San Rafacl | 150,980 |
| Santa Lucia | 18,679 |
| Santa Rosa | 13,787 |
| Sheep Mountain | 41,883 |
| Siskiyou | 152,680 |
| Snow Mountain | 36,370 |
| South Sierra | 82,084 |
| South Warner | 70,614 |
| Thousand Lakes | 16,335 |
| Trinity Alps | 498,141 |
| Ventana | 164,178 |
| Yolla Bolly-Middle Eel | 146,696 |

## Colorado

| | |
|---|---|
| Big Blue | 98,463 |
| Cache La Poudre | 9,238 |
| Collegiate Peaks | 166,716 |
| Comanche Peak | 66,791 |
| Eagles Nest | 133,325 |
| Flat Tops | 235,035 |
| Holy Cross | 122,388 |
| Hunter Fryingpan | 74,399 |
| Indian Peaks | 70,374 |
| La Garita | 103,986 |
| Lizard Head | 41,189 |
| Lost Creak | 105,090 |
| Maroon Bells-Snowmass | 180,962 |
| Mount Evans | 74,401 |
| Mount Massive | 27,980 |
| Mount Sneffels | 16,505 |
| Mount Zirkel | 139,818 |
| Neota | 9,924 |
| Never Summer | 13,757 |
| Platte River | 743 |
| Raggeds | 59,519 |
| Rawah | 73,068 |
| South San Juan | 127,690 |
| Weminuche | 459,604 |
| West Elk | 176,172 |

## Florida

| | |
|---|---|
| Alexander Springs | 7,700 |
| Big Gum Swamp | 13,600 |
| Billies Bay | 3,120 |
| Bradwell Bay | 24,602 |
| Juniper Prairie | 13,260 |
| Little Lake George | 2,500 |
| Mud Swamp/New River | 7,800 |

## Georgia

| | |
|---|---|
| Big Frog | 83 |
| Brasstown | 11,195 |
| Cohutta | 35,247 |
| Ellicott Rock | 2,181 |
| Raven Cliffs | 8,562 |
| Rich Mountain | 9,489 |
| Southern Nantahala | 12,439 |
| Tray Mountain | 9,702 |

# WILDERNESS AREAS

## Idaho

| | |
|---|---|
| Frank Church-River of No Return | 2,364,541 |
| Gospel Hump | 205,764 |
| Hells Canyon | 83,811 |
| Sawtooth | 227,088 |
| Selway-Bitterroot | 1,089,017 |

## Indiana

| | |
|---|---|
| Charles C. Dean | 12,935 |

## Kentucky

| | |
|---|---|
| Beaver Creek | 4,756 |
| Clifty | 12,427 |

## Louisiana

| | |
|---|---|
| Kisatchie | 8,700 |

## Michigan

| | |
|---|---|
| Big Island Lake | 5,840 |
| Delirium | 11,870 |
| Horseshoe Bay | 3,790 |
| Machinac | 12,230 |
| McCormick | 16,850 |
| Nordhouse Dunes | 3,450 |
| Rock River Canyon | 4,640 |
| Round Island | 378 |
| Sturgeon River Gorge | 14,500 |
| Sylvania | 18,327 |

## Minnesota

| | |
|---|---|
| Boundary Waters Canoe Area | 799,276 |

## Mississippi

| | |
|---|---|
| Black Creek | 5,012 |
| Leaf | 994 |

## Missouri

| | |
|---|---|
| Bell Mountain | 8,977 |
| Devils Backbone | 6,595 |
| Hercules-Glades | 12,314 |
| Irish | 16,117 |
| Paddy Creek | 7,019 |
| Piney Creek | 8,087 |
| Rockpile Mountain | 4,089 |

## Montana

| | |
|---|---|
| Absaroka-Beartooth | 920,327 |
| Anaconda-Pintlar | 157,874 |
| Bob Marshall | 1,009,356 |
| Cabinet Mountains | 94,272 |
| Gates of the Mountains | 28,562 |
| Great Bear | 286,700 |
| Lee Metcalf | 248,944 |
| Mission Mountains | 73,877 |
| Rattlesnake | 32,844 |
| Scapegoat | 239,296 |
| Selway-Bitterroot | 251,443 |
| Welcome Creek | 28,135 |

## Nebraska

| | |
|---|---|
| Soldier Creek | 7,794 |

## Nevada

| | |
|---|---|
| Arc Dome | 115,000 |
| Alta Toquima | 38,000 |
| Boundary Peak | 10,000 |
| Curant Mountain | 36,000 |
| East Humboldt | 36,900 |
| Grant Range | 50,000 |
| Jarbidge | 113,167 |
| Mount Charleston | 43,000 |
| Mount Moriah | 82,000 |
| Mount Rose | 28,000 |
| Quinn Canyon | 27,000 |
| Ruby Mountains | 90,000 |
| Santa Rosa - Paradise Peak | 31,000 |

Table Mountain    98,000

## New Hampshire

| Great Gulf | 5,552 |
| Pemigewasset | 45,000 |
| Presidential Range | |
|   -Dry River | 27,380 |
| Sandwich Range | 25,000 |

## New Mexico

| Aldo Leopold | 202,016 |
| Apache Kid | 44,626 |
| Blue Range | 29,304 |
| Capitan Mountains | 34,658 |
| Chama River Canyon | 50,300 |
| Cruces Basin | 18,000 |
| Dome | 5,200 |
| Gila | 557,873 |
| Latir Peak | 20,000 |
| Manzano Mountain | 36,875 |
| Pecos | 223,333 |
| San Pedro Parks | 41,132 |
| Sandia Mountains | 37,877 |
| Wheeler Peak | 19,661 |
| White Mountain | 48,208 |
| Withington | 19,000 |

## North Carolina

| Birkhead Mountains | 4,790 |
| Catfish Lake South | 7,600 |
| Ellicott Rock | 3,930 |
| Joyce Kilmer- | |
|   Slickrock | 13,132 |
| Linville Gorge | 10,975 |
| Middle Prong | 7,900 |
| Pocosin | 11,000 |
| Pond Pine | 1,860 |
| Sheep Ridge | 9,540 |
| Shining Rock | 18,450 |
| Southern Nantahala | 12,096 |

## Oklahoma

| Blackfork Mountain | 4,583 |
| Upper Kiamichi | 9,691 |

## Oregon

| Badger Creek | 24,000 |
| Black Canyon | 13,400 |
| Boulder Creek | 19,100 |
| Bridge Creek | 5,400 |
| Bull of the Woods | 34,900 |
| Columbia | 39,000 |
| Cummins Creek | 9,173 |
| Diamond Peak | 54,185 |
| Drift Creek | 5,798 |
| Eagle Cap | 358,461 |
| Gearhart Mountain | 22,809 |
| Grassy Knob | 17,200 |
| Hells Canyon | 130,095 |
| Kalmiopsis | 179,700 |
| Menagerie | 4,800 |
| Middle Santiam | 7,500 |
| Mill Creek | 17,400 |
| Monument Rock | 19,650 |
| Mount Hood | 46,520 |
| Mount Jefferson | 107,008 |
| Mount Thielsen | 55,100 |
| Mount Washington | 52,738 |
| Mountain Lakes | 23,071 |
| North Fork John Day | 121,352 |
| North Fork Umatilla | 20,435 |
| Red Buttes | 3,750 |
| Rock Creek | 7,400 |
| Rogue-Umpqua | |
|   Divide | 33,200 |
| Salmon-Huckleberry | 44,560 |
| Sky Lakes | 116,300 |
| Strawberry Mountain | 68,700 |
| Three Sisters | 285,202 |
| Waldo Lake | 39,200 |
| Wenaha-Tucannon | 66,375 |
| Wild Rogue | 25,658 |

# WILDERNESS AREAS

## Pennsylvania

| | |
|---|---|
| Allegheny Islands | 368 |
| Hickory Creek | 8,570 |

## South Carolina

| | |
|---|---|
| Ellicott Rock | 2,809 |
| Hell Hole Bay | 2,180 |
| Little Wambaw Swamp | 5,154 |
| Wambaw Creek | 1,937 |
| Wambaw Swamp | 4,767 |

## South Dakota

| | |
|---|---|
| Black Elk | 9,824 |

## Tennessee

| | |
|---|---|
| Bald River Gorge | 3,721 |
| Big Frog | 7,986 |
| Big Laurel Branch | 6,251 |
| Citico Creek | 16,226 |
| Cohutta | 1,795 |
| Gee Creek | 2,493 |
| Joyce Kilmer-Slickrock | 3,832 |
| Little Frog Mountain | 4,684 |
| Pond Mountain | 6,625 |
| Sampson Mountain | 8,319 |
| Unaka Mountain | 4,700 |

## Texas

| | |
|---|---|
| Big Slough | 3,584 |
| Indian Mounds | 10,917 |
| Little Lake Creek | 3,810 |
| Turkey Hill | 5,286 |
| Upland Island | 12,423 |

## Utah

| | |
|---|---|
| Ashdown Gorge | 7,000 |
| Box-Death Hollow | 25,751 |
| Dark Canyon | 45,000 |
| Deseret Peak | 25,500 |
| High Uintas | 456,705 |
| Lone Peak | 30,088 |
| Mount Naomi | 44,350 |
| Mount Nebo | 28,000 |
| Mount Olympus | 16,000 |
| Mount Timpanogos | 10,750 |
| Pine Valley Mountain | 50,000 |
| Twin Peaks | 11,334 |
| Wellsville Mountain | 23,850 |

## Vermont

| | |
|---|---|
| Big Branch | 6,720 |
| Breadloaf | 21,480 |
| Bristol Cliffs | 3,738 |
| George D. Aiken | 5,060 |
| Lye Brook | 15,503 |
| Peru Peak | 6,920 |

## Virginia

| | |
|---|---|
| Barbours | 5,600 |
| Beartown | 6,043 |
| James River Face | 9,086 |
| Kimberling Creek | 5,580 |
| Lewis Fork | 5,802 |
| Little Dry Run | 3,400 |
| Little Wilson Creek | 3,855 |
| Mountain Lake | 8,253 |
| Peters Mountain | 3,326 |
| Ramseys Draft | 6,725 |
| Rich Hole | 6,450 |
| Rough Mountain | 9,300 |
| Saint Mary's | 10,090 |
| Shawvers Run | 3,605 |
| Thunder Ridge | 2,344 |

## Washington

| | |
|---|---|
| Alpine Lakes | 362,621 |
| Boulder River | 48,674 |
| Buckhorn | 44,258 |
| Clearwater | 14,598 |
| Colonel Bob | 11,961 |
| Glacier Peak | 572,338 |

# WILDERNESS AREAS

| | |
|---|---|
| Glacier View | 3,123 |
| Goat Rocks | 104,641 |
| Henry M. Jackson | 92,673 |
| Indian Heaven | 20,960 |
| Lake Chelan-Sawtooth | 151,435 |
| Mount Adams | 46,626 |
| Mount Baker | 117,528 |
| Mount Skokomish | 13,015 |
| Noisy-Diobsud | 14,133 |
| Norse Peak | 51,343 |
| Pasayten | 530,031 |
| Salmo-Priest | 41,335 |
| Tatoosh | 15,750 |
| The Brothers | 16,682 |
| Trapper Creek | 5,970 |
| Wenaha-Tucannon | 111,048 |
| William O. Douglas | 168,288 |
| Wonder Mountain | 2,349 |

## West Virginia

| | |
|---|---|
| Cranberry | 35,864 |
| Dolly Sods | 10,215 |
| Laurel Fork North | 6,055 |
| Laurel Fork South | 5,997 |
| Mountain Lake | 2,500 |
| Otter Creek | 20,000 |

## Wisconsin

| | |
|---|---|
| Blackjack Springs | 5,886 |

| | |
|---|---|
| Headwaters | 18,108 |
| Porcupine Lake | 4,250 |
| Rainbow | 6,583 |
| Whisker Lake | 7,345 |

## Wyoming

| | |
|---|---|
| Absaroka-Beartooth | 23,283 |
| Bridger | 428,087 |
| Cloud Peak | 189,039 |
| Encampment River | 10,124 |
| Fitzpatrick | 198,525 |
| Gros Ventre | 287,000 |
| Huston Park | 30,588 |
| Jedediah Smith | 123,451 |
| North Absaroka | 350,488 |
| Platte River | 22,749 |
| Popo Agie | 101,870 |
| Savage Run | 14,940 |
| Teton | 585,238 |
| Washakie | 704,274 |
| Winegar Hole | 10,715 |

This list contains only forest service wilderness areas and is current as of 1989. Additional information for the State of Nevada came directly from P.L. 101-195.

# Cajun Style Fish and Rice

Steve Comeaux, 15 seasons,
Dry Creek Wilderness

*16 oz. of fish fillets*
*1 lg. onion*
*4 oz. butter*
*2-3 cloves of garlic*
*1 tsp. salt*
*1 tbsp. red pepper*
*3 tbsp. black pepper*
*1 c. dry white wine, optional*
*4 c. white rice*
*water*

Cook rice in water. Dice onion and garlic and brown in butter over medium heat for 10 min. Add 1/2 c. water (or wine) and seasonings to onion and garlic mixture. Cover and simmer on low heat for 30 min., stirring occasionally. Add fish, cover and simmer for an additional 10 min. Don't overcook. Serve over rice. Serves 3.

## Ute Lake Tacos

Scott Edwards, 3 seasons,
Weminuche Wilderness

6 blue corn tortillas
1 c. sharp cheddar cheese
1/2 to 1 lb. ground beef
salsa to taste
1-2 tbsp. cooking oil
4 green onions, chopped
cumin, garlic, chili powder to taste

Cook ground beef. Add seasonings. Pour oil into small pan and heat. Fill each tortilla with beef, onions and cheese. Fold over into a sandwich. Fry both sides for about 1 min. Remove from pan. Drain on paper towel or cloth. Add salsa to taste and serve.

**Note:** Ground beef can also be cooked at home and sealed in an airtight container. It will last for about 5 days.

**Variation:** Add diced cooked potatoes to meat mixture.

"Some of my fondest memories growing up are of wild areas that my father took me to and worked in. I would like to see future generations enjoy the benefits of seeing these wild areas in their original, pristine state. Through education and preservation, we can assure the areas stay that way."
- **Scott Edwards, Creede, CO**

"We must relate to the wilderness as though it must be in as good or better shape for the 101st generation as for this one. Err in favor of the environment. We must work locally for a global network of wilderness and protected areas to sustain species' diversity and life itself and work toward a sustainable development for the planet as a whole."
**- Michael Olwyler, North Fork, CA**

# Simple Mountain Bulgar

Michael Olwyler, 14 seasons,
Ansel Adams Wilderness

*1 c. bulgar wheat*
*1/2 pkg. Knorr's Minestrone Soup mix*
*2 1/3 c. water*
*1 sm. zucchini*
*1 sm. carrot*
*1 sm. can of chicken in water, optional*
*1 clove of garlic, smashed*

Combine Knorr's soup mix with water and bring to a boil. Pour in bulgar wheat and garlic. Stir. Bring mixture back to a boil. Turn stove on low, cover and let cook for 12 min. Listen to ensure that it doesn't burn. Add veggies and chicken and cook another 4-5 min. until done. Add more water as needed. The more variety of veggies you add, the more tasty the recipe.

## Pine:

• Pine needles are rich in vitamin C, and they are pleasant to chew on. Or steep them in boiling water and drink a tea that smells like Christmas.

# Whole Grain Baking Mix

Barbara Hartman, 4 seasons,
Cloud Peak Wilderness

2 c. all purpose flour
2 c. whole wheat flour
3/4 c. dry milk powder
1/2 c. quick-cooking oats
1/2 c. cornmeal
2 tbsp. baking powder
1 tsp. salt
1 c. shortening

"Doing my part has been a personal commitment for me. Hopefully the people I meet in my classes and as a ranger will learn no-trace skills. If these people go away caring more deeply about the wilderness and its future, I have done my job."
- **Barbara Hartman, Buffalo, WY**

**To prepare at home:** In large container, thoroughly combine dry ingredients. Using a pastry blender, blend in shortening until evenly dispersed. Store tightly covered, up to 2 weeks at room temperature or up to several months in the refrigerator.

**Whole Grain Biscuits:** 1 c. mix, 1/3 c. water. Mix just until moistened. Drop dough by spoonfuls on greased skillet, cover and cook 10-12 min. Makes 6 biscuits.

**Whole Grain Crust Pizza:** Soften 1/2 pkg. active dry yeast in 1/4 c. warm water. Stir in 1 c. mix. Knead 25 strokes, let rest 10 min. Grease skillet. Pat crust onto bottom of pan, build up edges. Cook 10 min. Spread 4 oz. pizza sauce on crust, sprinkle with desired toppers. Top with cheese. Cook 10 min. or until cheese is melted. **Hint:** Put heat diffuser between skillet and flame to keep bottom from overcooking.

# Cous-cous Menagerie

Mary Beth Hennessy, 5 seasons,
Ansel Adams Wilderness

"What I like most about being a ranger is waking up at first light. It's that first beam hitting the highest ridge above me. That's my alarm clock. I lean over on my side, reach to fire up my stove and brew up a morning cup. Watching the light change, I cheer on another day in the mountains."
- **Mary Beth Hennessy, Lee Vining, CA**

*3:1 ratio of cous-cous to boiling water*
*1 pkg. Knorr brand dried tomato-basil soup*
*1/8-1/4 c. powdered milk*
*1 can of clams or oysters*
*1 c. fresh veggies, any kind*
*2 cloves of garlic*
*basil, marjoram to taste*
*Parmesan cheese*

Add cous-cous to boiling water, cover and remove from heat. Let sit for 10 min. Combine other ingredients in separate pot and heat on stove. When warm, add to cous-cous. Sprinkle with Parmesan cheese and enjoy.

# Upside Down Pizza

Koji Kawamura, 2 seasons,
Maroon Bells-Snowmass Wilderness

*2 1/2 c. flour*
*1 tbsp. yeast*
*1 c. lukewarm water*
*dash of salt*
*1 tbsp. oil*
*1 tsp. sugar*
*1 c. tomato sauce*
*1 lb. mozarella cheese*
*1 c. mushrooms*

"Let us all work together to protect this fragile environment so posterity, too, may gaze on the borders of beauty herself."
- **Koji Kawamura, Aspen, CO**

Dissolve the sugar, salt and oil in lukewarm water (100°). Dissolve yeast into water solution. Let stand 5 minutes. Mix flour in until it's not sticky and knead well. Let dough rise about 15 min. Flatten dough and cook it on a low flame in skillet. Turn over and cook the other side until a light brown. Set aside. In skillet, add cheese and mushrooms, or any other pizza toppings. Add tomato sauce. Place crust on top of sauce. Cook for 10 min. on a low flame or until cheese browns. Flip over and let stand for a few min. before serving.

**Variation:** Use a packet of spaghetti sauce mix with tomato paste instead of tomato sauce.

# DINNER

## Veggie Spaghetti

Kenneth M. Brink Jr., 4 seasons,
Rawah Wilderness

*2 pkg. ramen noodles*
*1 sm. zucchini*
*1 sm. onion*
*1 sm. can of tomato paste*
*1 tsp. Italian herbs*
*1/2 tsp. garlic powder*
*water*

Start by thinly slicing the zucchini squash and thinly chopping the onion. Boil the noodles and zucchini together until cooked. Drain all but about 1/2 c. of the water and add spices, tomato paste and onions. Stir and heat as desired. Makes 2 servings.

**Walk softly on the land...
Leave No Trace**

# Quesa Noché (Cheese Night)

S. Bud Solmonsson, 5 seasons,
Trinity Alps Wilderness

*3-6 flour tortillas*
*1/2 lb. cheese of choice*
*1 onion*
*1 bell pepper*
*salsa to taste, optional*

Cook tortilla over medium heat in pan. Sprinkle chopped onions, bell peppers and salsa over one half of tortilla while it is cooking. Then put cheese over the same half, on top of ingredients. As soon as cheese starts to melt, fold the untouched tortilla half over to make a half circle. Turn the quesa noché over until all cheese is melted and serve.

**Note:** If served for lunch or breakfast, this will not be a quesa noché, but rather a quesa dia (cheese day).

"As humans, we have created anthropocentric rights; it took little time to learn how to abuse those rights in relation to wilderness. Wilderness, the natural occurring ecosystems, is like earth's child - innocent and naive."
**- S. Bud Solmonsson, Weaverville, CA**

# Crab and Cheese Curry

Lise Hall, 10 seasons,
Flat Tops Wilderness

*1/3 c. powdered milk*
*1-2 c. water*
*1 1/2 tbsp. butter*
*1 1/2 tbsp. flour*
*1 1/2 tsp. curry powder*
*dash of salt*
*2 dashes of pepper*
*4 oz. crab flakes*
*4 oz. cheese*
*1/4 c. rice*

Mix the powdered milk and 1 c. water. Set aside. Cook rice and set aside. Melt butter in a medium pan. Stir in flour to create a paste. Slowly stir in milk. Heat for a few minutes then add spices and cheese. When cheese has partially melted, stir in crab flakes. (Keep crab frozen until ready to leave for trip. It will last 2 or 3 days.) Heat until hot. Serve over rice. Serves 2.

# Coyote Lake Zucchini

Greg Marks, 5 seasons,
John Muir Wilderness

*2 zucchini*
*1 sm. can tomato sauce - can substitute*
     *1 pkg. of tomato soup mix*
*1 pkg. onion soup mix*
*1 1/2 c. minute rice*
*1 c. grated cheese - use your favorite*
*water*

Slice zucchini and place in pot with tomato sauce. Mix in onion soup mix and 1/2 c. water. Let this simmer at low heat until zucchini are tender. In another pot, prepare minute rice according to directions. Once zucchini is tender and rice is done, mix all the ingredients of two pots together. Add grated cheese, mix evenly and chow down.

"The wilderness is very fragile and we must manage it closely. Some say, 'Leave it alone. It will take care of itself.' This may have been true years ago when the use was minimal, but today, the wilderness is taking a beating. It must be managed for future generations to enjoy so they can say, 'I'm in the wilderness, an unspoiled area unlike any other on earth.'"
**- Greg Marks, Shaver Lake, CA**

## Wilderness management:

• Wilderness is intended for the use and enjoyment of the American people. But we share an obligation to leave it as we found it, in its natural condition, for the pleasure of future visitors.

# Chicken and Dumplings

Terry Carlson, 4 seasons,
Comanche Peak Wilderness

*1 c. flour*
*2 tsp. baking powder*
*1/4 c. powdered milk*
*2 tbsp. vegetable oil*
*1 sm. can of chicken*
*1 stalk of celery, chopped*
*1 carrot, chopped*
*1/2 onion, chopped*
*salt, thyme, oregano, basil, pepper,*
    *parsley, sage to taste*
*4 1/2 c. water*

**Dumplings:** Mix flour, baking powder, milk and salt together. Add 1/2 c. water and oil and mix until moistened.

**Chicken Broth:** Combine chicken, celery, carrot, onion and spices with 4 c. water. Bring to a boil. Reduce heat. Drop dumpling dough by spoonfuls into broth and simmer until dumplings are cooked. Makes 2 servings.

**Variations:** Add zucchini, chili powder, green chili or cabbage to chicken broth. Substitute ramen or veggie noodles for the dumplings.

# Dandelion Salad

### Karl F. Zeller, 6 seasons, Cache La Poudre Wilderness

*6 c. young, tender dandelion leaves*
*4 slices bacon*
*2 tbsp. vinegar*
*2 tbsp. brown sugar*
*1/4 tsp. salt*
*1 tbsp. lemon juice, optional*
*1 hard boiled egg, optional*

Cook bacon over stove. When done, remove and cool grease. Add vinegar, lemon juice, sugar and salt to bacon grease and heat slowly while stirring. Pour hot bacon dressing over washed and dried dandelion greens. Add chopped egg and crumbled bacon to top and eat as you watch the clouds roll by.

**Variation:** Add 2 tbsp. sour cream and one beaten raw egg to grease before reheating.

"I like the feel of clean air making its way into and out of my body. The idea of preserving and protecting the wildness, including the air resource of certain areas, appeals to me. I support the wilderness concept to insure that myself, my children and your children can breathe free at any cost."
**- Karl F. Zeller, Bellvue, CO**

## Dandelions:

• The young leaves of this familiar **weed** are good in soups and salads. The older leaves need cooking - and butter, salt and pepper. Wine is made from the heads of the plant.

# Linguini and Clams

Barbara Walker, 3 seasons,
High Uintas Wilderness

*1/2 c. olive oil*
*1/2 tsp. pepper*
*1/2 c. Parmesan cheese*
*1 tsp. oregano*
*2 tbsp. basil*
*3 cloves of garlic (1 tsp. dried)*
*6 oz. can of clams*
*3 tbsp. parsley*
*1/2 c. dried mushrooms*
*1 tbsp. dried onion*
*16 oz. linguini noodles*
*water*

Reconstitute onions and mushrooms in water for a few minutes. Drain. Sauté onions and mushrooms in oil. Add herbs and seasonings. Pour in juice from can of clams. Simmer for 15-20 min. while cooking noodles in water. When mushrooms are tender, add clams and Parmesan cheese. Remove from heat and serve with noodles.

# Max and Louise

Rik Smith, 5 seasons,
Glacier Peak Wilderness

*1 qt. water*
*2 c. pasta noodles*
*1/4-1/2 lb. cheese, cheddar, jack,*
*    mozzarella, or any combo*
*1/2 c. nuts*
*1/2 c. onions*
*garlic, the more the merrier*
*salt, soy sauce, oregano, basil, chili*
*    powder, cumin, cayenne, black*
*    pepper and cinnamon to taste*

Prepare the pasta using a minimum of water so that you don't have to pour any out (after a day on the trail you need the water, and there's all the good pasta juices in it) but still have some standing water over the noodles. The onions, whether fresh or dehydrated, should be added to the water with the pasta.

When the pasta is ready, add the cheese, nuts and garlic. While the cheese is melting, add spices to taste. Makes 1 serving.

The key to this meal, as with all wilderness meals, is to freely adapt the recipe to the supplies you have in your pack.

"In the way spotted owls are an indicator of the health of an old growth western hemlock or douglas fir ecosystem, wilderness is an indicator of the health of the planetary ecosystem. Therefore, wilderness (Congressionally designated) needs to be managed in such a way that it retains its wilderness qualities, purity and health."
- **Rik Smith, Darrington, WA**

> " We have reached the last of our remaining undeveloped lands of this country. I want those remaining lands protected for their natural inherent values now and in the future, for the survival of this country and the world as a whole."
>
> **- Gordon Ash, Hungry Horse, MT**

# Old World Chicken

Gordon Ash, 9 seasons,
Bob Marshall Wilderness

*1 lb. chicken, cut into small pieces*
*1/4 tsp. curry powder*
*1/4 tsp. garlic powder*
*1/4 tsp. sage*
*1/4 tsp. oregano*
*1/4 tsp. poultry seasoning*
*1/4 tsp. onion powder*
*8 oz. bottle of soy sauce*
*1 tsp. margarine or vegetable oil*

Put chicken pieces in large pan, greased lightly with margarine or vegetable oil. Add spices and soy sauce. Cook over medium heat until done.

# Sheep Herder Potatoes

Ricky E. Brazell, 1 season,
High Uintas Wilderness

*1 can whole potatoes*
*1 can evaporated milk*
*salt, pepper and garlic powder to taste*
*flour, optional*

Drain the water off the canned potatoes and dump them into a pan over medium high heat. With a spatula, start cutting the potatoes as they fry. Once heated, add can of milk and let it start to simmer. Don't let the pan get too hot or the milk will scorch. Add seasonings to taste. Add flour for thickening if desired. Serves 2.

"By crossing the wilderness boundary, I can get away from the stress of the world and enter a land untouched by man and observe wildlife in its natural habitat. Likewise I want to insure that this legacy will be around for my three sons. I want them to know that they can go back to the wilderness and see it the same way I did when I was there."
**Ricky E. Brazell, Duchesne, UT**

## Tips for desert camping:

- Water means life in the desert; don't be without it!
- Carry plenty of water - at least 1 gallon per person per day in warm weather.
- Heat exhaustion and heat stroke are serious problems. To avoid them, drink lots of water and avoid extreme exertion during the heat of the day.
- Use care when hiking on slickrock (especially if wet). Sandstone is soft and fractures easily. Sand grains can act like ball bearings under your shoes.
- Don't camp in dry streambeds. Flash floods can occur at any time of the year but they are most common during the late summer thunderstorm season.
- Stay on designated trails. Avoid damaging fragile cryptobiotic soil (a dark, crusty covering on the sand) by staying on slickrock when exploring off-trail. An area of mature cryptobiotic may take 100 years to develop, but can be destroyed by just a few steps.

"Use but don't abuse the wilderness. These truly magnificent areas are a reminder to me of the awesomeness of our Lord who has control of our world."
- **Ronald E. Wilcox, Laramie, WY**

# Fish Chowder

Ronald E. Wilcox, 8 seasons,
Savage Run Wilderness

*6 sm. trout*
*1 medium onion*
*6 carrots*
*6 potatoes*
*6 stalks of celery*
*10 oz. can of corn*
*salt, pepper to taste*
*1/4 c. flour*
*1/4 c. powdered milk*
*garlic to taste, optional*
*a pinch of parsley flakes*
*water*

Clean and peel raw vegetables. Chop them into small pieces and add to pot of boiling water. Cook until tender. In a separate pot, boil the cleaned and beheaded trout for 10 minutes. Remove trout (save cooking broth) and let fish cool. Once cool, skin trout and remove bones. When vegetables are tender, add fish, reserved fish broth, can of corn and seasonings to taste. Combine flour with powdered milk in a pint jar. Shake well. Add to vegetable mixture, stirring constantly until chowder thickens to desired consistency. Serve with crackers or hot biscuits. Serves 6.

# Cous-cous with Veggies

Jill Shoemaker, 1 season,
Otter Creek Wilderness

*1 box of cous-cous*
*1 c. vegetables, any kind*
*1 clove of garlic, chopped*
*butter, salt and pepper to taste*
*water*

"I never realized how exciting wilderness management could be. If we humans keep it simple, Mother Nature will handle the complexities."
**- Jill Shoemaker, Petersburg, WV**

Boil vegetables in water. Add garlic and cous-cous. Remove from heat. Once water is absorbed by cous-cous, season with butter, salt and pepper.

**Variations:**
- Add can of turkey, chicken or tuna after vegetables are boiled.
- Season with soy sauce or Tamari.
- Add nuts, raisins and maple syrup and eat hot or cold for breakfast.

> "Wilderness is our ancestral home in a neighborhood where there is no doubt that we belong. It is important to go home to remember what we as a species like to forget - that we don't have all the answers."
> - Jonathan W. Klein, Ennis, MT

# Packer's Peppers Magnifique

Jonathan W. Klein, 8 seasons,
Lee Metcalf Wilderness

*1 whole green pepper (gutted) per
  person*
*1 pkg. Near East brand wheat pilaf*
*1 handful of raisins*
*1/2 c. green onions*
*5-6 large slices of favorite cheese
  per person*
*garlic powder to taste*
*lemon pepper to taste*

Place pilaf, raisins, onions and spices in large pot. Cook pilaf according to directions. Place whole green peppers on top of pilaf mixture while cooking so that they can be steamed soft by the time the pilaf is done (about 25 min. boiling time). When done, stuff the pepper with alternating layers of pilaf and cheese until pepper is bulging. Top with more cheese and eat.

## Preserving archaeological sites:

- If you find Indian artifacts, pictographs or petroglyphs, show your respect by leaving them alone.
- Don't camp in Indian ruins.
- Save America's past for the future - report Indian artifact violations to the National Parks and Conservation Association, 1-800-448-NPCA.

# Tortilla Pizza

John Baas, 3 seasons,
Lake Chelan-Sawtooth Wilderness

*3/4 c. water*
*6 oz. can tomato paste*
*1 tbsp. oregano*
*1 tbsp. basil*
*1 tbsp. thyme*
*1 tbsp. garlic*
*1 tsp. cooking oil*
*1 c. grated mozzarella cheese*
*4 nine-inch whole wheat flour tortillas*
*1 c. pizza toppings of your choice*

Combine water with paste. Add spices and stir until consistency is uniform. Add more or less water depending on the desired thickness of sauce. Heat to boiling, stirring constantly, then set aside. Make sure skillet is well oiled. Put 2 tortillas together in skillet and cook over low heat until brown. Spread 1/2 sauce on top, add 1/2 toppings and 1/2 cheese, cover and cook 4 to 5 minutes or until cheese melts. Repeat for second set of tortillas. Makes 2 nine-inch pizzas.

"I became a wilderness ranger for the enhancement of my own psyche. The success of wilderness management in the future will depend on a ranger's ability to effectively monitor resource conditions."
**- John Baas, Chelan, WA**

> "Wild forever....
> let's keep it
> that way."
> - D. L. Dowell,
> Hamilton, MT

# Cous-cous and Chicken

D. L. Dowell, 8 seasons,
Selway-Bitterroot Wilderness

*1 pkg. instant cous-cous with dried
 vegetables*
*4 oz. can of chicken*
*Tabasco to taste*
*water*

Boil cous-cous with enough water to cover. When water is absorbed, add chicken, Tabasco and any other seasonings.

---

## Memorable words in wilderness:

"I'm glad I shall never be young without wild country to be young in."

**- Aldo Leopold,** wilderness advocate

# Miller's Beef Jerky

Mason C. Miller Jr., 6 seasons,
Caney Creek Wilderness

*24 oz. flank steak*
*3/4 c. red wine*
*1/3 c. Worcestershire sauce*
*1/2 c. soy sauce*
*1 tsp. salt or seasoned salt, optional*
*1 tsp. onion powder*
*1/2 tsp. garlic powder*
*1/4 tsp. pepper, optional*
*1/2 onion, sliced*
*3/4 c. water or more to dilute taste*

**To prepare at home:** Trim fat off of steak. Slice it along the grain into thin strips. Combine rest of ingredients. Add strips of meat, cover tightly and let sit, refrigerated, overnight. In the morning, drain off liquid and arrange meat strips over oven rack. Put foil below the meat to catch drips. Bake at 150° for 6 to 8 hours, leaving the oven door slightly open. Turn oven off and let jerky sit for about 2 more hours or until dry.

**Note:** Thickness of jerky determines cooking time. Use your own judgment.

**Storage:** Put jerky in a plastic bag, close it and poke several small holes in bag. Then put this bag into a second one and leave the top of the second bag open. Jerky can also be frozen.

"One thing I've learned is that it's best to start at the ground floor - work with the public to end up with a better product. We must work closely with them and not mislead them. The public must have ownership and involvement in the process of managing wilderness. Only then will our areas be better protected. "
- Mason C. Miller Jr., Mena, AR

"Wilderness belongs to all of us, not just those that manage the areas or those that live nearby or even those who visit. How devastating to our collective pysches not to have remote, "pristine" areas set aside to dream about and to explore in our minds, if not in person."
- **Lissa Fahlman, Petersburg, AK**

# High Bush Cranberry Tea

Lissa Fahlman, 10 seasons, Stikine-LeConte Wilderness

*1 handful highbush cranberries off nearest bush*
*dash of honey*
*flavored brandy, optional*
*water*

Place 8-10 cranberries in cup (best after the first frost. Berries can usually be found anytime of the year as a few will last over the winter). Pour boiling water over berries and add a taste of honey. Mash berries to release flavor. A small amount of brandy can be added as a nightcap. Watch out for seeds.

## Spearmint:

• The mild and delightful tea made from the leaves of this delicately fragrant plant has been used to treat many ailments and to alleviate the pain of childbirth.

## Paul Toddies

Kari Gunderson, 11 seasons,
Mission Mountains Wilderness

*1 tsp. Postum*
*1-2 tsp. hot chocolate mix*
*1 tsp. powdered milk*
*1 dash each of cinnamon and vanilla*
*water*

Mix dry ingredients. Boil 1 cup water. Add water to dry ingredients, stir and serve.

**Variation:** Add Ovaltine to taste.

"As the world population grows so does the lust for natural silence and space. Having the opportunity to experience the power of wilderness without the intrusion of others is truly the essence of what we seek from wilderness."
**Kari Gunderson, Condon, MT**

# Hell Canyon Brownies

Margaret Foster, 10 seasons,
Indian Peaks Wilderness

"Wilderness is where I've met the best friends of my life and it is a place where my spirit feels truly at home."
**- Margaret Foster, Granby, CO**

*1 c. unbleached flour*
*2 eggs*
*1 c. brown sugar*
*1/2 tsp. salt*
*1/4 c. margarine*
*8 oz. pkg. semisweet chocolate chips*
*6 oz. can frozen orange juice*
*1/4 c. coconut*
*1/2 c. walnuts*
*1 tsp. vanilla*

**To prepare at home:** Cream margarine, sugar and eggs. Add all other ingredients. Mix and spread into shallow, greased pan, 9"x9". Bake at 325° for 30-35 min. Cut into squares and seal in airtight container to take along on trip. These are guaranteed to get you up Hell Canyon and back in a day.

> "I love the scenery, fresh air and peaceful tranquility that the wilderness offers."
> **- Kathy Rydberg, Pecos, NM**

# Kathy's Magic Popcorn

Kathy Rydberg, 1 season,
Pecos Wilderness

*1/4 c. popcorn*
*1 1/2 tbsp. olive oil*
*1 1/2 tbsp. Brewer's yeast*
*salt to taste*

Pour oil into backpack pot. With 3 kernels of popcorn at the bottom and the cover on, turn stove on high. After the 3 kernels pop, pour the rest of the popcorn in. Just before popping stops, remove pot. Sprinkle Brewer's yeast over popcorn. Add salt if desired.

---

## Wildflowers:

- Wildflowers should be left for others to enjoy. The blue columbine, the Colorado state flower, can be identified by its blue and white flowers that tip upward at the ends of stems of bushy plants.

# Chocolate Tortillas

Penny Roeder, 7 seasons,
South San Juan Wilderness

*2 tortillas*
*24 oz. chocolate bar*
*1 tbsp. butter*

Heat butter in skillet. Add 1 tortilla and cook until lightly browned. Flip tortilla. Add grated or broken up chocolate according to personal taste. Cover skillet so chocolate will melt. Fold tortilla and enjoy. Repeat.

"Without wilderness we would lose touch with our oneness with nature. Taking care of the wilderness' enduring resources only helps to insure our species will endure."
- **Penny Roeder, Pagosa Springs, CO**

## How long it will last:
• How long will it last if you leave it behind?
- Orange peel: 3 months
- Paper container: 5 months
- Wool socks: 1 to 5 years
- Milk carton: 5 years
- Plastic bag: 20 years
- Nylon fabric: 30 to 40 years
- Plastic bottle: 50 to 80 years
- Aluminum can: 80 to 100 years (longer, if submerged)
          - courtesy of Missouri Department of Conservation

# Boy Scout Ice Cream

Frank S. Erickson, 6 seasons,
Eagle Cap Wilderness

"We must manage wilderness with the minimum amount of regulation needed to protect and preserve the resource while allowing wilderness users the greatest amount of personal freedom. Well-trained and well-informed wilderness rangers are the key to accomplishing this job."
- Frank S. Erickson, Enterprise, OR

*1 can Eagle Brand sweetened evaporated milk*
*1 can fruit pie filling (cherry and blueberry are my favorites)*
*fresh snow*

Start by placing about 2 quarts of clean snow in a 4-quart or larger bowl and pour in 1/2 of the milk. Mix the snow and milk together with a spoon (wooden ones work best) until the mixture has the consistency of ice cream. Adjust mixture by adding either milk or snow or both as needed. When the mixture is right, pour in the fruit. If things look a little runny, set the entire mixture outside the tent in the sub-zero temperatures. Eat as soon as possible. Makes enough to feed a small troop.

**Hint:** This recipe is best in the winter. Summer snow is usually too coarse and dirty to make ice cream.

# Backcountry Cheesecake

Linda Merigliano, 11 seasons,
Jedediah Smith Wilderness

*1 tbsp. margarine*
*1/3 c. milkman powdered milk mixed*
*with 1 1/3 c. water*
*1 box of Jello or Royal cheesecake mix*

In pan you want to make cheesecake in, melt margarine. Mix in cracker crumbs included in cheesecake mix. Add water to make stiff paste and press along bottom of pan. Combine milk with filling mix. Pour over crust. Set in cool place (snowbank is great) for about 15 min. Voila - instant cheesecake! Garnish with favorite strawberry or blueberry preserves.

"Being a wilderness ranger offers the opportunity to apply strong interests in managing resources on the ground and teaching and sharing information with others. It is a great combination of physical work and public interaction in an incredible setting."
- **Linda Merigliano, Driggs, ID**

# Backcountry Compote

Rachel Ondov, 1 season,
Lee Metcalf Wilderness

"Wilderness is a place where I can obtain a sense of serenity by becoming attuned to the earth. I enjoy being distinctly aware of the moon phases, the seasonal changes and wildlife habits. It keeps me humble and respectful as a human to remember that I am just another animal species. We need to listen to the earth for she has some valuable lessons for us to learn."
- Rachel Ondov, West Yellowstone, MT

*2-3 c. mixed or dried fruit*
*1 tbsp. cinnamon*
*1 c. whipped cream or yogurt*
*brown sugar or honey to sweeten*
*optional: almonds, sunflower seeds,*
*    coconut, trail mix, liquor (brandy*
*    is good), fresh fruit*
*water*

In a saucepan, cover the dried fruit with water. Cook til soft. Add sweetener, cinnamon and any optional ingredients (clean out your day pack!). Continue to simmer gently. Whipped cream or yogurt is mixed in or dolloped on top for garnish. Serve on pancakes or alone as dessert.

# Jello Salad

Connie Coulter, 1 season,
Frank Church-River of No Return Wilderness

*3 oz. pkg. jello mix (any flavor)*
*2 c. water*
*fruit (any kind)*
*1/2 c. trail mix, candy or nuts, optional*

Add 1 c. of boiling water and 1 c. cold water to jello. Add fruit and other filler as desired. Place in a pan or container that can be tightly covered. Put container in the creek for a few hours (or overnight) and salad will be set.

"The wilderness ranger is a vital link in the education of wilderness users. When more people see the wilderness as a place to cherish and harmonize with rather than conquer, we will be saving a wilderness that can be enjoyed for generations to come."
- **Connie Coulter, Garden Valley, ID**

# DESSERT

## Pistachio Pudding

Gayne Sears, 7 seasons,
High Uintas Wilderness

*1 box of instant pistachio pudding*
*2 c. cold water*
*3 tbsp. powdered milk (enough to make 2 c. of milk)*

Mix powdered milk with water in 1 quart water bottle. Add pudding mix. Shake vigorously for 2 min. Pour liquid into cups. Allow to set (time varies depending on outside temperature) and serve.

## Memorable words in wilderness:

"In wildness is the preservation of the world."
- **Henry David Thoreau,** philosopher and writer

# Fruit Soup

Anne S. Fege, 6 seasons,
Forest Service, Washington Office

2 qts. water
8 oz. dried apricots
8 oz. raisins
8 oz. pitted prunes
3 cinnamon sticks, broken into 2-3
    pieces each
2 c. juice, any kind
3 tbsp. cornstarch
whipped cream or yogurt, optional

Soak fruit overnight in water, if possible. Other dried fruit can also be added or substituted. The next day, bring water, fruit and cinnamon to boil and simmer until tender. Dissolve cornstarch in 1/2 c. juice. Add mixture plus the rest of the juice to soup and stir until thick. Serve either warm or cold. A spoonful of whipped cream or yogurt makes this an extra treat. Serves 8.

"Listen to the land and to the people who know and love that land. Be uncompromising in keeping wilderness free from long-term human impact, for that is the true value of wilderness."
- Anne S. Fege, Washington, D.C.

"I find beauty, peace, adventure and an acute ability to live in the moment only while being in the wilderness. There is plenty of developed land and not enough undeveloped land; thus the environmental concerns come first."
- Marilyn Krings, Pagosa Springs, CO

# Apricot/Peanut Delights

Marilyn Krings, 4 seasons,
Weminuche Wilderness

*1 pkg. dried apricots*
*8 oz. peanut butter*
*1 pkg. rice cakes*
*water*

Cut apricots into small pieces. Place in pan with enough water to barely cover fruit. Cook slowly until you have a warm, thick paste. Meanwhile, break each rice cake into 4 pieces. Smear with peanut butter. Cover with warm apricot puree and enjoy.

# Fruit Squares

Jim Ficke, 30 seasons,
Flat Tops Wilderness

*2 eggs*
*1/2 c. honey*
*2/3 c. flour*
*1 c. chopped pecans*
*1 c. chopped fruit (i.e. dried apricots,*
    *apples, pineapple, pears, raisins)*
*1/2 c. chocolate chips, optional*

**To prepare at home:** Mix eggs and honey. Add flour and mix. Blend in nuts, fruit and chocolate chips. Scrape into an oiled 8"x8" pan. Bake at 350° for 30 minutes or until the top begins to brown. Cut into squares and store in an airtight container for trip.

"I love the challenge, beauty and opportunity wilderness provides for everyone associated with it. I love to teach people how to use the wilderness and still protect and preserve it for future generations."
**- Jim Ficke, Steamboat Springs, CO**

## To begin an education program:

• Begin with previously tested material and tailor it to your area.
• Start with one or maybe two programs - one for children and one for adults.
• Develop each program for the audience you wish to reach.
• Practice your presentation, know the material and be professional.
• Look at the long term results as a way to better your area as well as the entire wilderness system.
        - courtesy of the Superstition Wilderness Education Program

## Cookstove Cake

Frank Beum, 4 seasons,
Weminuche Wilderness

*1 bag of Richmoor Sierra Coffee Cake Mix (or any other water-based cake mix)*
*1/2 c. water*
*1 large pot*
*1 small pot*

Line bottom of larger pot with one layer of small pebbles. Pour cake mix and water into smaller pot and mix until smooth. Place small pot inside of large pot (on top of pebbles). Cover and cook over low to medium heat for 15 min. or until the cake doesn't stick to a wooden match. Enjoy and then return pebbles where you found them.

# High Country Fry Bread

Laura Lantz, 7 seasons,
High Uintas Wilderness

2 c. flour
1 tsp. salt
1 tbsp. baking powder
1/2 tbsp. cooking oil
water
2-3 c. oil (enough to deep fry bread)

Mix dry ingredients. Add 1/2 tbsp. oil and enough water to make a stiff dough. Knead for 5 min. Roll into 3-inch balls and flatten each like a pancake. Cut thin lines from center to outside of pancake (in the shape of a star) so that air can get into the dough. Place this into heated oil in skillet. Cook until golden brown and crisp.

**Variation:** Top with refried beans and cheese, veggies and cheese or honey.

"Maintaining pristine areas to allow future generations a chance to share the beauty with us today is very rewarding. If properly managed, our love for the outdoors will be secured for this generation as well as many generations to come."
- **Laura Lantz,** Duchesne, UT

# Get involved...
# Become a
# Wilderness
# Volunteer

Volunteer to assist in maintaining trails, monitoring impacts, rehabilitating campsites, picking up litter, educating visitors to no trace techniques and much more. To make a difference in your area, contact your nearest public lands agency.

# SUGGESTED READINGS

To read more about backcountry cookery, wilderness and management of designated wildernesses, the following books are suggested:

*A Citizen's Guide to Wilderness Management.* Edited by F. Beum, S. Marsh and L. Ziemann. October 1990. The Wilderness Society, Washington D.C. 50 pages.

*Philosophy Gone Wild.* H. Rolston III. 1989. Prometheus Books, Buffalo, New York. 269 pages.

*Sand County Almanac.* A. Leopold. 1949. Oxford University Press, Inc., New York, New York. 295 pages.

*Soft Paths.* B. Hampton and D. Cole. 1988. NOLS. Stackpole Books, Harrisburg, Pennsylvania. 173 pages.

*The Complete Walker III. The Joys and Techniques of Hiking and Backpacking.* 3rd Ed. C. Fletcher. 1989. A. A. Knopf, Inc., New York, New York. 668 pages.

*The NOLS Cookery.* 2nd Ed. S. Richard, D. Orr, and C. Lindholm. 1988. NOLS Publication, Lander, Wyoming. 104 pages.

*Wilderness and the American Mind.* R. Nash. 1982. Yale University Press, New Haven, Connecticut. 425 pages.

*Wilderness Management Report of Society of American Foresters.* Wilderness Management Task Force. 1989. Society of American Foresters, Bethesda, Maryland. 85 pages.

*Wilderness Medicine.* 3rd Ed. W. Forgey, M.D. 1987. ICS Books, Inc., Merrillville, Indiana. 151 pages.

---

**To learn more:** A Wilderness Management Correspondence Study Course is offered by Colorado State University Department of Recreation Resources in Fort Collins, Colorado. For more information, contact Ralph Swain, 303-498-1057.

# WILDERNESS ACT

Public Law 88-577
88th Congress, S. 4
September 3, 1964

## An Act

To establish a National Wilderness Preservation System for the permanent good of the whole people, and for other purposes.

*Be it enacted by the Senate and House of Representatives of the United States of America in Congress assembled,*

### SHORT TITLE

SECTION 1. This Act may be cited as the "Wilderness Act".

### WILDERNESS SYSTEM ESTABLISHED STATEMENT OF POLICY

SEC. 2. (a) In order to assure that an increasing population, accompanied by expanding settlement and growing mechanization, does not occupy and modify all areas within the United States and its possessions, leaving no lands designated for preservation and protection in their natural condition, it is hereby declared to be the policy of the Congress to secure for the American people of present and future generations the benefits of an enduring resource of wilderness. For this purpose there is hereby established a National Wilderness Preservation System to be composed of federally owned areas designated by Congress as "wilderness areas", and these shall be administered for the use and enjoyment of the American people in such manner as will leave them unimpaired for future use and enjoyment as wilderness, and so as to provide for the protection of these areas, the preservation of their wilderness character, and for the gathering and dissemination of information regarding their use and enjoyment as wilderness; and no Federal lands shall be designated as "wilderness areas" except as provided for in this Act or by a subsequent Act.

(b) The inclusion of an area in the National Wilderness Preservation System notwithstanding, the area shall continue to be managed by the Department and agency having jurisdiction thereover immediately before its inclusion in the National Wilderness Preservation System unless otherwise provided by Act of Congress. No appropriation shall be available for the payment of expenses or salaries for the administration of the National Wilderness Preservation System as a separate unit nor shall any appropriations be available for additional personnel stated as being required solely for the purpose of managing or administering areas solely because they are included within the National Wilderness Preservation System.

### DEFINITION OF WILDERNESS

(c) A wilderness, in contrast with those areas where man and his own works dominate the landscape, is hereby recognized as an area where the earth and its community of life are untrammeled by man, where man himself is a visitor who does not remain. An area of wilderness is further defined to mean in this Act an area of undeveloped Federal land retaining its primeval character and influence, without permanent improvements or human habitation, which is protected and managed so as to preserve its natural conditions and which (1) generally appears to have been affected primarily by the forces of nature, with the imprint of man's work substantially unnoticeable; (2) has outstanding opportunities for solitude or a primitive and unconfined type of recreation; (3) has at least five thousand acres of land or is of sufficient size as to make practicable its preservation and use in an unimpaired condition; and (4) may also contain ecological, geo-

# WILDERNESS ACT

logical, or other features of scientific, educational, scenic, or historical value.

### NATIONAL WILDERNESS PRESERVATION SYSTEM—EXTENT OF SYSTEM

SEC. 3. (a) All areas within the national forests classified at least 30 days before the effective date of this Act by the Secretary of Agriculture or the Chief of the Forest Service as "wilderness", "wild", or "canoe" are hereby designated as wilderness areas. The Secretary of Agriculture shall—

(1) Within one year after the effective date of this Act, file a map and legal description of each wilderness area with the Interior and Insular Affairs Committees of the United States Senate and the House of Representatives, and such descriptions shall have the same force and effect as if included in this Act : *Provided, however*, That correction of clerical and typographical errors in such legal descriptions and maps may be made.

(2) Maintain, available to the public, records pertaining to said wilderness areas, including maps and legal descriptions, copies of regulations governing them, copies of public notices of, and reports submitted to Congress regarding pending additions, eliminations, or modifications. Maps, legal descriptions, and regulations pertaining to wilderness areas within their respective jurisdictions also shall be available to the public in the offices of regional foresters, national forest supervisors, and forest rangers.

(b) The Secretary of Agriculture shall, within ten years after the enactment of this Act, review, as to its suitability or nonsuitability for preservation as wilderness, each area in the national forests classified on the effective date of this Act by the Secretary of Agriculture or the Chief of the Forest Service as "primitive" and report his findings to the President. The President shall advise the United States Senate and House of Representatives of his recommendations with respect to the designation as "wilderness" or other reclassification of each area on which review has been completed, together with maps and a definition of boundaries. Such advice shall be given with respect to not less than one-third of all the areas now classified as "primitive" within three years after the enactment of this Act, not less than two-thirds within seven years after the enactment of this Act, and the remaining areas within ten years after the enactment of this Act. Each recommendation of the President for designation as "wilderness" shall become effective only if so provided by an Act of Congress. Areas classified as "primitive" on the effective date of this Act shall continue to be administered under the rules and regulations affecting such areas on the effective date of this Act until Congress has determined otherwise. Any such area may be increased in size by the President at the time he submits his recommendations to the Congress by not more than five thousand acres with no more than one thousand two hundred and eighty acres of such increase in any one compact unit ; if it is proposed to increase the size of any such area by more than five thousand acres or by more than one thousand two hundred and eighty acres in any one compact unit the increase in size shall not become effective until acted upon by Congress. Nothing herein contained shall limit the President in proposing, as part of his recommendations to Congress, the alteration of existing boundaries of primitive areas or recommending the addition of any contiguous area of national forest lands predominantly of wilderness value. Notwithstanding any other provisions of this Act, the Secretary of Agriculture may complete his review and delete such area as may be necessary, but not to exceed seven thousand acres, from the southern tip of the Gore Range-Eagles Nest Primitive Area,

# WILDERNESS ACT

Colorado, if the Secretary determines that such action is in the public interest.

(c) Within ten years after the effective date of this Act the Secretary of the Interior shall review every roadless area of five thousand contiguous acres or more in the national parks, monuments and other units of the national park system and every such area of, and every roadless island within, the national wildlife refuges and game ranges, under his jurisdiction on the effective date of this Act and shall report to the President his recommendation as to the suitability or nonsuitability of each such area or island for preservation as wilderness. The President shall advise the President of the Senate and the Speaker of the House of Representatives of his recommendation with respect to the designation as wilderness of each such area or island on which review has been completed, together with a map thereof and a definition of its boundaries. Such advice shall be given with respect to not less than one-third of the areas and islands to be reviewed under this subsection within three years after enactment of this Act, not less than two-thirds within seven years of enactment of this Act, and the remainder within ten years of enactment of this Act. A recommendation of the President for designation as wilderness shall become effective only if so provided by an Act of Congress. Nothing contained herein shall, by implication or otherwise, be construed to lessen the present statutory authority of the Secretary of the Interior with respect to the maintenance of roadless areas within units of the national park system.

(d)(1) The Secretary of Agriculture and the Secretary of the Interior shall, prior to submitting any recommendations to the President with respect to the suitability of any area for preservation as wilderness—

(A) give such public notice of the proposed action as they deem appropriate, including publication in the Federal Register and in a newspaper having general circulation in the area or areas in the vicinity of the affected land;

(B) hold a public hearing or hearings at a location or locations convenient to the area affected. The hearings shall be announced through such means as the respective Secretaries involved deem appropriate, including notices in the Federal Register and in newspapers of general circulation in the area: *Provided*, That if the lands involved are located in more than one State, at least one hearing shall be held in each State in which a portion of the land lies;

(C) at least thirty days before the date of a hearing advise the Governor of each State and the governing board of each county, or in Alaska the borough, in which the lands are located, and Federal departments and agencies concerned, and invite such officials and Federal agencies to submit their views on the proposed action at the hearing or by no later than thirty days following the date of the hearing.

(2) Any views submitted to the appropriate Secretary under the provisions of (1) of this subsection with respect to any area shall be included with any recommendations to the President and to Congress with respect to such area.

(e) Any modification or adjustment of boundaries of any wilderness area shall be recommended by the appropriate Secretary after public notice of such proposal and public hearing or hearings as provided in subsection (d) of this section. The proposed modification or adjustment shall then be recommended with map and description thereof to the President. The President shall advise the United States Senate and the House of Representatives of his recommendations with respect to such modification or adjustment and such recom-

# WILDERNESS ACT

mendations shall become effective only in the same manner as provided for in subsections (b) and (c) of this section.

### USE OF WILDERNESS AREAS

SEC. 4. (a) The purposes of this Act are hereby declared to be within and supplemental to the purposes for which national forests and units of the national park and national wildlife refuge systems are established and administered and—

(1) Nothing in this Act shall be deemed to be in interference with the purpose for which national forests are established as set forth in the Act of June 4, 1897 (30 Stat. 11), and the Multiple-Use Sustained-Yield Act of June 12, 1960 (74 Stat. 215).

(2) Nothing in this Act shall modify the restrictions and provisions of the Shipstead-Nolan Act (Public Law 539, Seventy-first Congress, July 10, 1930; 46 Stat. 1020), the Thye-Blatnik Act (Public Law 733, Eightieth Congress, June 22, 1948; 62 Stat. 568), and the Humphrey-Thye-Blatnik-Andresen Act (Public Law 607, Eighty-fourth Congress, June 22, 1956; 70 Stat. 326), as applying to the Superior National Forest or the regulations of the Secretary of Agriculture.

(3) Nothing in this Act shall modify the statutory authority under which units of the national park system are created. Further, the designation of any area of any park, monument, or other unit of the national park system as a wilderness area pursuant to this Act shall in no manner lower the standards evolved for the use and preservation of such park, monument, or other unit of the national park system in accordance with the Act of August 25, 1916, the statutory authority under which the area was created, or any other Act of Congress which might pertain to or affect such area, including, but not limited to, the Act of June 8, 1906 (34 Stat. 225; 16 U.S.C. 432 et seq.) ; section 3(2) of the Federal Power Act (16 U.S.C. 796(2)) ; and the Act of August 21, 1935 (49 Stat. 666; 16 U.S.C. 461 et seq.).

(b) Except as otherwise provided in this Act, each agency administering any area designated as wilderness shall be responsible for preserving the wilderness character of the area and shall so administer such area for such other purposes for which it may have been established as also to preserve its wilderness character. Except as otherwise provided in this Act, wilderness areas shall be devoted to the public purposes of recreational, scenic, scientific, educational, conservation, and historical use.

### PROHIBITION OF CERTAIN USES

(c) Except as specifically provided for in this Act, and subject to existing private rights, there shall be no commercial enterprise and no permanent road within any wilderness area designated by this Act and, except as necessary to meet minimum requirements for the administration of the area for the purpose of this Act (including measures required in emergencies involving the health and safety of persons within the area), there shall be no temporary road, no use of motor vehicles, motorized equipment or motorboats, no landing of aircraft, no other form of mechanical transport, and no structure or installation within any such area.

# WILDERNESS ACT

### SPECIAL PROVISIONS

(d) The following special provisions are hereby made:

(1) Within wilderness areas designated by this Act the use of aircraft or motorboats, where these uses have already become established, may be permitted to continue subject to such restrictions as the Secretary of Agriculture deems desirable. In addition, such measures may be taken as may be necessary in the control of fire, insects, and diseases, subject to such conditions as the Secretary deems desirable.

(2) Nothing in this Act shall prevent within national forest wilderness areas any activity, including prospecting, for the purpose of gathering information about mineral or other resources, if such activity is carried on in a manner compatible with the preservation of the wilderness environment. Furthermore, in accordance with such program as the Secretary of the Interior shall develop and conduct in consultation with the Secretary of Agriculture, such areas shall be surveyed on a planned, recurring basis consistent with the concept of wilderness preservation by the Geological Survey and the Bureau of Mines to determine the mineral values, if any, that may be present; and the results of such surveys shall be made available to the public and submitted to the President and Congress.

(3) Notwithstanding any other provisions of this Act, until midnight December 31, 1983, the United States mining laws and all laws pertaining to mineral leasing shall, to the same extent as applicable prior to the effective date of this Act, extend to those national forest lands designated by this Act as "wilderness areas"; subject, however, to such reasonable regulations governing ingress and egress as may be prescribed by the Secretary of Agriculture consistent with the use of the land for mineral location and development and exploration, drilling, and production, and use of land for transmission lines, waterlines, telephone lines, or facilities necessary in exploring, drilling, producing, mining, and processing operations, including where essential the use of mechanized ground or air equipment and restoration as near as practicable of the surface of the land disturbed in performing prospecting, location, and, in oil and gas leasing, discovery work, exploration, drilling, and production, as soon as they have served their purpose. Mining locations lying within the boundaries of said wilderness areas shall be held and used solely for mining or processing operations and uses reasonably incident thereto; and hereafter, subject to valid existing rights, all patents issued under the mining laws of the United States affecting national forest lands designated by this Act as wilderness areas shall convey title to the mineral deposits within the claim, together with the right to cut and use so much of the mature timber therefrom as may be needed in the extraction, removal, and beneficiation of the mineral deposits, if needed timber is not otherwise reasonably available, and if the timber is cut under sound principles of forest management as defined by the national forest rules and regulations, but each such patent shall reserve to the United States all title in or to the surface of the lands and products thereof, and no use of the surface of the claim or the resources therefrom not reasonably required for carrying on mining or prospecting shall be allowed except as otherwise expressly provided in this Act: *Provided*, That, unless hereafter specifically authorized, no patent within wilderness areas designated by this Act shall issue after December 31, 1983, except for the valid claims existing on or before December 31, 1983. Mining claims located after the effective date of this Act within the boundaries of wilderness areas designated by this Act shall create no rights in excess of those rights which may be patented under the

# WILDERNESS ACT

provisions of this subsection. Mineral leases, permits, and licenses covering lands within national forest wilderness areas designated by this Act shall contain such reasonable stipulations as may be prescribed by the Secretary of Agriculture for the protection of the wilderness character of the land consistent with the use of the land for the purposes for which they are leased, permitted, or licensed. Subject to valid rights then existing, effective January 1, 1984, the minerals in lands designated by this Act as wilderness areas are withdrawn from all forms of appropriation under the mining laws and from disposition under all laws pertaining to mineral leasing and all amendments thereto.

(4) Within wilderness areas in the national forests designated by this Act, (1) the President may, within a specific area and in accordance with such regulations as he may deem desirable, authorize prospecting for water resources, the establishment and maintenance of reservoirs, water-conservation works, power projects, transmission lines, and other facilities needed in the public interest, including the road construction and maintenance essential to development and use thereof, upon his determination that such use or uses in the specific area will better serve the interests of the United States and the people thereof than will its denial; and (2) the grazing of livestock, where established prior to the effective date of this Act, shall be permitted to continue subject to such reasonable regulations as are deemed necessary by the Secretary of Agriculture.

(5) Other provisions of this Act to the contrary notwithstanding, the management of the Boundary Waters Canoe Area, formerly designated as the Superior, Little Indian Sioux, and Caribou Roadless Areas, in the Superior National Forest, Minnesota, shall be in accordance with regulations established by the Secretary of Agriculture in accordance with the general purpose of maintaining, without unnecessary restrictions on other uses, including that of timber, the primitive character of the area, particularly in the vicinity of lakes, streams, and portages: *Provided*, That nothing in this Act shall preclude the continuance within the area of any already established use of motorboats.

(6) Commercial services may be performed within the wilderness areas designated by this Act to the extent necessary for activities which are proper for realizing the recreational or other wilderness purposes of the areas.

(7) Nothing in this Act shall constitute an express or implied claim or denial on the part of the Federal Government as to exemption from State water laws.

(8) Nothing in this Act shall be construed as affecting the jurisdiction or responsibilities of the several States with respect to wildlife and fish in the national forests.

### STATE AND PRIVATE LANDS WITHIN WILDERNESS AREAS

Sec. 5. (a) In any case where State-owned or privately owned land is completely surrounded by national forest lands within areas designated by this Act as wilderness, such State or private owner shall be given such rights as may be necessary to assure adequate access to such State-owned or privately owned land by such State or private owner and their successors in interest, or the State-owned land or privately owned land shall be exchanged for federally owned land in the same State of approximately equal value under authorities available to the Secretary of Agriculture: *Provided, however*, That the United States shall not transfer to a State or private owner any mineral interests unless the State or private owner relinquishes or

# WILDERNESS ACT

causes to be relinquished to the United States the mineral interest in the surrounded land.

(b) In any case where valid mining claims or other valid occupancies are wholly within a designated national forest wilderness area, the Secretary of Agriculture shall, by reasonable regulations consistent with the preservation of the area as wilderness, permit ingress and egress to such surrounded areas by means which have been or are being customarily enjoyed with respect to other such areas similarly situated.

(c) Subject to the appropriation of funds by Congress, the Secretary of Agriculture is authorized to acquire privately owned land within the perimeter of any area designated by this Act as wilderness if (1) the owner concurs in such acquisition or (2) the acquisition is specifically authorized by Congress.

### GIFTS, BEQUESTS, AND CONTRIBUTIONS

_ SEC. 6. (a) The Secretary of Agriculture may accept gifts or bequests of land within wilderness areas designated by this Act for preservation as wilderness. The Secretary of Agriculture may also accept gifts or bequests of land adjacent to wilderness areas designated by this Act for preservation as wilderness if he has given sixty days advance notice thereof to the President of the Senate and the Speaker of the House of Representatives. Land accepted by the Secretary of Agriculture under this section shall become part of the wilderness area involved. Regulations with regard to any such land may be in accordance with such agreements, consistent with the policy of this Act, as are made at the time of such gift, or such conditions, consistent with such policy, as may be included in, and accepted with, such bequest.

(b) The Secretary of Agriculture or the Secretary of the Interior is authorized to accept private contributions and gifts to be used to further the purposes of this Act.

### ANNUAL REPORTS

SEC. 7. At the opening of each session of Congress, the Secretaries of Agriculture and Interior shall jointly report to the President for transmission to Congress on the status of the wilderness system, including a list and descriptions of the areas in the system, regulations in effect, and other pertinent information, together with any recommendations they may care to make.

**Approved September 3, 1964.**

LEGISLATIVE HISTORY:

HOUSE REPORTS: No. 1538 accompanying H. R. 9070 (Comm. on Interior & Insular Affairs) and No. 1829 (Comm. of Conference).
SENATE REPORT No. 109 (Comm. on Interior & Insular Affairs).
CONGRESSIONAL RECORD:
    Vol. 109 (1963): Apr. 4, 8, considered in Senate.
                Apr. 9, considered and passed Senate.
    Vol. 110 (1964): July 28, considered in House.
                July 30, considered and passed House, amended, in lieu of H. R. 9070.
                Aug. 20, House and Senate agreed to conference report.

# INDEX

# BE A NO TRACE CAMPER

For more information on the
**Leave No Trace!** ethic, call
1-800-332-4100.

# RECIPE NOTES

# RECIPE NOTES

# RECIPE NOTES

# ORDER FORM

# Order a book
# for a friend.

For additional copies of this cookbook, contact:
## San Juan National Forest Association
## P.O. Box 2261
## Durango, Colorado 81302
## or call: (303) 385-1210

Please mail me_____ copies of your Wilderness
Ranger Cookbook at $8.00 per copy plus $2.00 for
postage per book. Make checks payable to SJNFA.
Enclosed is my check or money order for _____.

Mail books to:

Name _____

Address_____

City, State, Zip_____

Please mail me_____copies of your Wilderness
Ranger Cookbook at $8.00 per copy plus $2.00 for
postage per book. Make checks payable to SJNFA.
Enclosed is my check or money order for _____.

Mail books to:

Name _____

Address_____

City, State, Zip_____